Uncle Jo

BATHROOM READER®

Germophobia

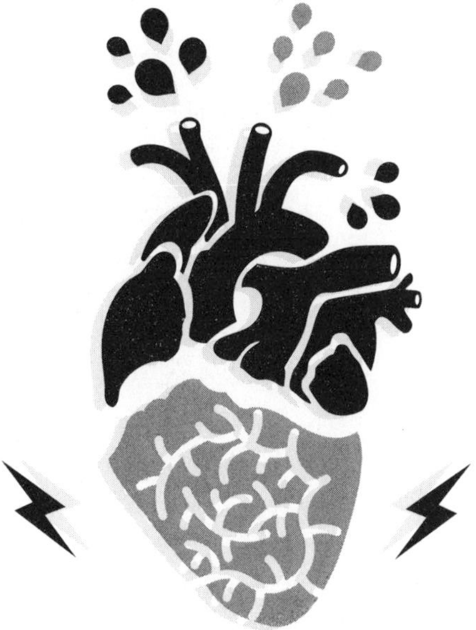

BATHROOM READERS' PRESS
ASHLAND, OREGON

"The material of contagions is a living one, and is indeed endowed with life, which is, in relation to the diseased body, a parasitic organism."

–German pathologist Friedrich Henle, supporting Louis Pasteur's theory that disease is spread by infectious germs, 1840

"A flu shot is the worst thing you can do. Because it's got mercury. If you have a flu shot for more than five years in a row, there's 10 times the likelihood that you'll get Alzheimer's disease.

–Comedian Bill Maher, 2007

UNCLE JOHN'S BATHROOM READER®

GERMOPHOBIA

For information, write: The Bathroom Readers' Institute,
P.O. Box 1117, Ashland, OR 97520
www.bathroomreader.com

Cover and interior design by Andy Taray / Ohioboy.com

ISBN-10: 1-60710-901-8 / ISBN-13: 978-1-60710-901-3

Library of Congress Cataloging-in-Publication Data

Uncle John's bathroom reader germophobia.

p. cm.

ISBN 978-1-60710-901-3 (pbk.)

1. Medicine--Miscellanea. 2. Medicine--History--Miscellanea. 3. Medical care--History--Miscellanea. 4. Curiosities and wonders. I. Bathroom Readers' Institute (Ashland, Or.) II. Title: Bathroom reader germophobia.

R706.U53 2013

610--dc23

2013023211

Printed in the United States of America
First Printing: April 2014
1 2 3 4 5 18 17 16 15 14

THANK YOU!

The Bathroom Readers' Institute sincerely thanks the people whose advice and assistance made this book possible.

Gordon Javna

Brian Boone

Andy Taray

Christy Taray

Trina Janssen

Joan Kyzer

Brandon Hartley

Megan Todd

Jack Feerick

Jon Cummings

Scott Eckert

Pablo Goldstein

Annie Zaleski

Matt Springer

Chris Holmes

Ben Godar

Eleanor Pierce

Lindsay Gillingham Taylor

Kim Griswell

Jay Newman

David Hoye

Blake Mitchum

Jennifer Frederick

Sydney Stanley

Lilian Nordland

Aaron Guzman

Dan Mansfield

Joseph Lister

CONTENTS

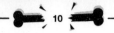

SANITIZE THIS!

There is nothing worse than getting sick... except the idea of having to go to the doctor when you get sick. So much can go wrong at the doctor, or the hospital, or the clinic. You could get a flesh-eating virus. Or they could give you the wrong medicine. Or too much medicine. Or decline your insurance. Or the doctor could tell you to eat more vegetables. (The horrors!)

Now Uncle John, the wizard of oddities, brings you *Germophobia*, a book for the health-obsessed, Purell-slathering, doctor-fearing patient inside all of us. What's so (darkly) funny about surgical tools being left inside patients, or all the weird diseases you could get? It's like a car wreck (or an ambulance crash)—you just can't look away.

All your fears are justified in *Germophobia*. Read about: doctors who spread deadly infections, doctors who were just pretending to be doctors in the first place, surgeons who removed the wrong part (or too many parts), horrific hospitals, medical mistakes, nasty nurses, and all those microscopic monsters who are hellbent on killing you (or at least on giving you diarrhea).

It'll make you sick (in a good way).

—The Bathroom Readers' Institute

WHOOPS, WRONG KIDNEY

Having a kidney problem is one of those nightmare illnesses that everybody dreads. Between the pain, a potential lifetime of dialysis, and a kidney-transplant list that can leave you waiting up to a decade for a vital organ, living a life with kidney issues is hardly living at all. But can you imagine having a tragic cherry placed on top of the ice cream sundae that is your faulty kidneys?

Unluckily for a patient at Park Nicollet Methodist Hospital in St. Louis Park, Minnesota, that is exactly what happened. The patient had checked into the hospital in 2008 to undergo surgery for a cancerous kidney. But it wasn't until a day after the surgery that doctors realized they had removed the patient's lone, healthy kidney. Safeguards, including marking the skin over body parts and "time-outs" to allow surgeons to double-check what they're cutting into, were in place at this hospital to ensure the patient's safety. But somehow they were missed before the incision and removal were made.

The surgeon who made the error voluntarily stepped down from seeing patients until an investigation was complete. But that was little comfort to the patient, who was now left with zero healthy kidneys and a history of cancer...which makes most people ineligible for a transplant.

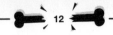

GERM FACTS YOU DON'T WANT TO KNOW

There are an average of 70,000 germs on a typical toilet seat. That sounds like a lot, but it's a relatively low number. A cutting board in your kitchen has about 140,000 germs. Your keyboard? About 300,000 germs. The bottom of your shoe boasts about 400,000 germs. A faucet: about 1.1 million germs. An escalator handrail: 2.8 million. Your desk at work: around 9 million. And worst of all, a well-used kitchen sponge for "cleaning" your dishes is approximately 200,000 times as germ-infested as a toilet seat. That's roughly 14 billion germs you're spreading around to your spoons and forks.

• Telephones get handled a lot, so they're predictably dirty–around 500,000 germs in all. Surprisingly, landline telephone handsets are incubators of worse germs than smartphones. A University of London study found that a quarter of landline phones tested positive for bacteria that lead to skin rashes and respiratory disease. Only 3 percent of touch-screen phones tested positive.

• How many hospitals are compliant with local health-department handwashing standards? About 40 percent.

• A third of all doorknobs have cold germs on them.

• Germs can live on most surfaces for up to two days.

• Washing your clothes doesn't exactly kill harmful germs so much as it spreads them. An underwear-only load of laundry contains around 100 million *E. coli* cells, which can survive and thrive in the hot, moist environment of a washing machine and then spread to the next load of clothes, or towels, or sheets. Basically, if you have a "sanitary" setting on your washer, use it when you wash your underwear (and maybe everything else, too).

• It's not surprising to learn that toothbrushes have bacteria on them. After all, they live in the bathroom, and that's also where people poop. But this statistic isn't about toothbrushes in use—50 percent of toothbrushes *still in the package* are laden with bacteria.

• Public transit is better for the health of the planet, but not so much yours. According to a 2011 study by the University of Nottingham, people who use public transit for their daily commute to work are six times more likely to contract a cold or the flu than those who drive or bike to work.

• Your body sheds about 10 million skin cells every day. There is ten times that much bacteria living on your skin every day. That represents more than 100 different kinds of bacteria.

• Taking it all into consideration—viruses, bacteria, and other pathogens and contagions—there are more germs on your body than there are people in the United States.

LEFT BEHIND

Now where did that roll of gauze go?" is the last thing you'd want to hear after waking up from surgery, but unfortunately, the situation referred to as a "retained surgical item" happens more often than you'd think. That's when a sponge, needle, or other surgical instrument is left inside of a person after a procedure (by accident, of course).

Studies suggest it happens somewhere between 4,500 and 6,000 times a year in the United States alone. In 70 percent of these incidents, sponges and gauze used to soak up excess blood are left behind. Ten percent are needles. *Needles.* Five percent are classified as "instruments," meaning scalpels.

Some horrifying examples of surgical souvenirs that patients didn't ask for:

• In February 2010, a foot-long metal pipe was removed from a Czechoslovakian woman five months after she obtained it in a different surgery.

• In 2010, Air Force major Erika Parks suffered extreme pain and swelling in her abdomen following an emergency C-section. Her stomach continued to grow after the birth, however, before doctors discovered a sponge entangled within her intestines. It took six hours to remove all of the infected tissue and particles of sponge, which had begun to break down.

• In 2006, 43-year-old Lenny LeClair sought medical

treatment after he noticed that his constant case of projectile vomiting smelled like feces. A CT scan revealed that several sponges had been left in LeClair's abdominal cavity following a surgery the year before. The infection destroyed part of his colon, and his intestines were so ravaged that parts of them had to be removed. Now he wears a colostomy bag.

Surely there is some way for hospitals to avoid such grievous errors? There is. Sponges and other instruments can be embedded with a radio frequency tag. Before stitching up a wound, surgeons can use a sensor to scan the patient's body for strays. The technology is used in only about 25 percent of American hospitals...even though it adds only $8 to $12 to the cost of a surgery.

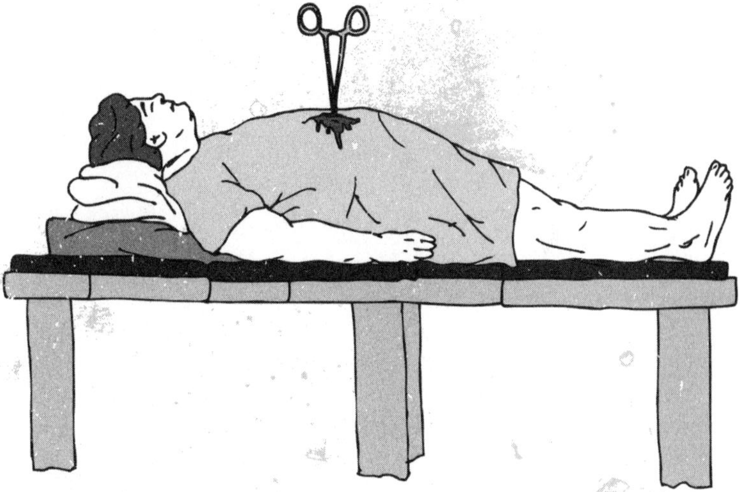

PHARMACY PHOLLIES

According to the *Journal of the American Pharmacists Association*, pharmacies make over 50 million mistakes every year–that's four mistakes per pharmacy, per day. So if you're currently taking any medications…maybe you shouldn't read this.

Motrin might kill you. In 2001 a mother went to a Walgreens in Colorado to pick up some prescription-strength Motrin (ibuprofen) for her two-year-old. Instead, she was accidentally given Levetiracetam, a medication that controls epilepsy. It also causes breathing problems in some people, such as those with asthma…like the woman's son. Breathe easy: She noticed the mix-up before it was too late.

Something in the water. A CVS pharmacy in New Jersey routinely filled prescriptions for fluoride pills for several children. (Yes, most communities have fluoridated water, but dentists prescribe fluoride supplements to kids with dental problems or who are just bad at brushing their teeth.) But for five months in 2011 and 2012, the kids were instead given Tamoxifen, a breast cancer drug. That won't be coming out of your faucet anytime soon.

B_{13}? Cyanocobalamin, also known as vitamin B_{12}, is prescribed to patients with a deficiency or difficulty absorbing that nutrient. But when a Washington, D.C., woman picked up her injectable cyanocobalamin prescription, she was surprised to find atropine instead.

You probably haven't heard of it—unless you've had nerve-gas poisoning, since that's what it treats. If you don't have nerve-gas poisoning, cyanocobalamin can, you know, poison you. (Again, the patient noticed the mistake before taking the wrong medication.)

A handful of these mistakes are unavoidable. But as the number of new drugs grows, systemic errors are likely to increase. This is because there are more and more drugs with similar, easily confusable names. The Institute for Safe Medication Practices says there are now over 700 such similar-sounding drugs.

Tramadol/Trazodone. After an alarming number of mix-ups, the Oregon Board of Pharmacy issued a formal warning about these two drugs. One is for insomnia, the other for extreme pain.

Materna/Matulane. Materna is a common prenatal vitamin. Matulane is a chemotherapy drug used to treat Hodgkin's lymphoma, designed specifically to slow cell growth and DNA development. In other words, not something you want near a growing fetus. At least one lawsuit claimed that the mistaken use of Matulane instead of Materna caused the patient to miscarry.

Kapidex/Casodex. Kapidex is for GERD, a severe gastrointestinal condition. Casodex treats prostrate cancer. Among the latter's possible side effects is, ironically, severe gastrointestinal problems (also liver failure). Because of complications caused by these repeated replacements, the FDA ordered Kapidex to change its name—it's now called Dexilant.

IT'S SNOT WHAT YOU THINK

A lot can go wrong with the human body, but some problems are definitely worse than others. A broken leg, a massive head wound, blood in the urine–those are the kinds of things you might want to have a professional take a look at. A runny nose? Big deal. You've got a cold or some hay fever. It'll go away on its own in a few days.

That's what Joe Nagy thought about his runny nose. He woke up one morning in 2012 with a few drops of clear liquid coming out of his nose. That happened once or twice a week, and Nagy thought it was allergies (although he lives in Phoenix, which is built on a desert, where there isn't a lot of pollen). But the dripping continued, with the flow growing to teaspoon-size puddles dropping out of his nose. After 18 months of this–*18 months*–Nagy decided to see a doctor.

An examination showed that it wasn't snot coming out of Nagy's nose. No, there was a hole in the membrane surrounding his brain, and every day for the past year and a half, brain fluid had been leaking out of his nose. The body makes and uses about 12 ounces a day; it had been constantly replenishing, then leaking out, every day for 18 months.

The hole was easily fixed with surgery. But still, if you've had a runny nose for a year or more, maybe go to the doctor–just in case it's your brain trying to slowly escape.

KIDNEY VS. GALLBLADDER

It's been a long time since we played Operation, but we do remember that it was kind of a big deal that if you were supposed to remove the patient's bread basket, you didn't take out the heart instead. For most of us, that's as far as our medical training went. Well, that and the fact that there isn't actually a bucket-shaped organ in the knee.

But we expect more from actual surgeons, which is why the 2006 case of Dr. Patrick M. McEnaney is so frightening. Dr. McEnaney was set to remove the gallbladder from an 84-year-old woman's body in a laparoscopic surgery. When the good doctor encountered unexpected inflammation, he switched to an open procedure and duly removed her…right kidney. It is unclear why Dr. McEnaney, who is a doctor, thought that that would do the trick.

"HE WAS SET TO REMOVE THE GALLBLADDER AND THEN DULY REMOVED… HER RIGHT KIDNEY."

The error was not discovered until a pathologist tested the organ three days later. Presumably, Dr. McEnaney figured he was in the clear when the patient's nose didn't flash red and she didn't make a buzzing noise.

FOOL ME THRICE...

Not that we'd know, but being a brain surgeon is probably one of the more stressful occupations out there. Even when you're performing a "routine" surgery, it's always a serious situation when the brain is involved. Every decision the surgeon makes can have a life-altering impact on a patient, from which size blade to use, to how deep to cut, to whether or not he cuts into the correct side of the head.

Yes. One must always cut into the correct side of the head. It's the first thing they teach at Brain Surgeon Academy.

In 2007, doctors at Rhode Island Hospital in Providence started treating patients' noggins like their own personal piñatas. Three times that year, surgeons cut into the wrong side of their patients' heads–twice getting all the way through the skull before realizing their mistake. This in spite of safety procedures like preoperative checklists and the use of markers to draw big Xs, making it explicitly clear where they're supposed to cut.

After the third incident, the hospital was fined $50,000, because the Rhode Island Department of Health frowns upon that sort of thing.

SEW WHAT?

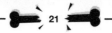

In 1993 Gennady Varlamov of Ekaterinburg, Russia, went to the doctor because he had a bad headache. (In countries with government-sponsored health care, you can go to the doctor when you have a bad headache.) The doctor could find nothing besides minor flu symptoms, so he took an X-ray of Varlamov's head, fearing signs of a tumor, aneurysm, or another scary thing.

He found three sewing needles.

"My hair stood on end when I saw the X-ray," Varlamov said. "This is incredible that I have had them all my life!" They were 1½ to 3 inches long, at the top of his brain just beneath the skull.

The doctor recommended not removing them surgically, since they had clearly posed no danger to Varlamov for all the time they had been in his head. For how long? Nobody knows for sure. Nor does Varlamov have any idea how the needles got there. What's weirder is that the headache was unrelated to the needles and went away on its own.

What's really weirder is that this story wasn't made public until 13 years later. In 2006 Varlamov's local TV station offered a free television to a viewer with the most interesting story. Varlamov won with the old "There are three sewing needles in my head and I don't know how they got there" story.

KIDNEY, BEEN

Imagine for a moment that you're a nurse in the operating room. You decide to tidy up a little. Used surgical instruments? Let's get those cleaned and sanitized. Garbage cans? Yup, better empty those. How about that perfectly functional organ sitting right there waiting to be implanted in another person? Toss that right out like a half-eaten burger.

Actually, don't do that last one. That just might get you into trouble. We know this because in 2012, Paul Fudacz Jr. went under the knife to make one of the ultimate sacrifices for a loved one—he was set to donate one of his kidneys to his ailing sister, Sarah.

The removal was a success, and Paul's kidney was sitting in a slush machine (not the same as a Slushee machine; it keeps the organ moist and fresh), waiting to be implanted. That's when a nurse walked in and threw the entire contents of the machine down the medical waste chute.

The kidney was found, but since it was covered in poop, blood, and other nasty substances, it was not used. The good news is Sarah got another healthy kidney. The hospital got a healthy lawsuit, and the nurse got a pink slip.

PRESCRIPTION: MRMRMFETRYGJVX

It's a cliché that doctors have terrible handwriting—they have to take extensive notes quickly and so can't always be legible. But that can be a real problem with prescriptions. Due to unknown abbreviations, writing too small, or unclear dosage instructions, an estimated 7,000 people die each year due to handwriting-related prescription errors.

In 2011, Dalia Hernandez, 72, was admitted to Northeast Baptist Hospital in San Antonio to have a toe amputated. She was also a dialysis patient, so to keep her kidneys in check, kidney specialist Dr. Flavio Alvarez prescribed 10 millimoles of potassium. After surgeons had to remove Hernandez's entire foot, Alvarez upped the potassium dose to 20 millimoles. Except he didn't write a new prescription—he just wrote over the "1" with a "2." Hospital pharmacists took that to mean "120" millimoles. That's a fatal dose, and it killed Hernandez.

In 1995 cardiologist Ramachandra Kolluru prescribed for his patient Ramon Vasquez 20 milligrams of Isordil, a medicine that would relieve his angina. But to Vasquez's pharmacist, "Isordil" looked a lot like "Plendil," which is a drug that lowers blood pressure. Vasquez, a heart patient, really didn't need to have his blood pressure lowered. The dose of Plendil killed him.

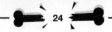

TOO MUCH, TOO LITTLE, TOO LATE

In 2002 a Burbank, California, man named Joe Deocampo checked into Providence St. Joseph Medical Center after he experienced some alarming symptoms. An ER doctor diagnosed Deocampo as having suffered a mild heart attack. People almost always survive mild heart attacks with no lasting damage.

Not so for Deocampo. But then, it wasn't the heart attack that permanently altered his quality of life–it was his medical treatments at Providence St. Joseph that did.

The doctor ordered an MRI for Deocampo and even wrote "stat" on the request, which means "emergency." Then he gave Deocampo a blood thinner, standard procedure that makes for more accurate MRI results. But the blood thinner worked too well, and Deocampo suffered excruciating back pain and spinal bleeding. And all the while, he was still waiting for the MRI. In all, he waited eight hours–clearly writing "stat" on a chart doesn't mean much in a crowded, understaffed hospital.

After those eight hours, Deocampo was finally up for his MRI, which is when doctors discovered the spinal bleeding. But it was too late–the combination of damage from an untreated heart attack and unattended spinal bleeding left Deocampo permanently paralyzed from the waist down.

THE ACCIDENTAL HEART PATIENT

You ever start a new job and find out someone in the office has a name similar to yours? It can get pretty annoying, right? All that mail belonging to you, Alex Johnson, keeps getting delivered to Alec Johannson. Well at least in that case, it's a letter from HR and not invasive heart surgery.

Unfortunately for Joan Morris, a 67-year-old patient undergoing an angiogram for her brain aneurysm, she happened to be recuperating in the same hospital as a 77-year-old patient named Jane Morrison. If you couldn't guess by now, Joan wasn't in the hospital for the same reason as Jane. After a successful angiogram, the patient is usually well enough to be discharged within 24 hours. But because of their similar names, Joan was wheeled into the operating room reserved for Jane and given an invasive cardiac electrophysiology procedure.

In layman's terms, the doctors made an incision by her groin and snaked a tube through her body and into her heart. Luckily for Joan, doctors realized the error, stopped the procedure, and returned her to her room in stable condition.

As for Jane? Let's just hope there wasn't a Joanne Marris in the room next door.

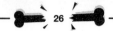

YOU ARE MORE LIKELY TO DIE IF...

You have surgery during the wrong moon cycle. In a 2013 study, researchers found that patients who had a type of heart surgery called aortic dissection repair had shorter hospital stays and were significantly less likely to die if they had their surgery during the waning full-moon period of the lunar cycle—that's just after a full moon.

You're a patient at an overcrowded ER. A study examined California hospitals that were routinely so overcrowded they diverted ambulances elsewhere. Patients at those overcrowded ERs were 5 percent more likely to die.

The nurse treating you has more patients. One study found that risk-adjusted patient death over a 30-day period was 7 percent higher for each additional patient per nurse.

You have an elective surgery on the weekend. Researchers at the Imperial College of London analyzed millions of procedures that occurred between 2008 and 2011 and found that the day of the week you have an elective surgery affects your risk of death greatly. Monday is the best day to avoid the Grim Reaper, and the risk of death increases every day of the week that passes. The increased risk of death on the weekend—an astounding 82 percent.

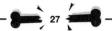

You take a multivitamin. Studies are increasingly finding higher death rates for people, specifically women, who take multivitamins. Often, even healthier women–those who smoke and drink less, as well as those who aren't obese–are more likely to die if they take multivitamins.

Your doctor is older. In one 2005 study, researchers found surgeons over the age of 60 tend to have higher death rates among patients than those aged 41 to 50, even though they tend to perform fewer procedures. Even younger, presumably less-experienced surgeons below the age of 40 tend to have comparable patient death rates to the 41-50 group. Another found that the higher the number of years since medical-school graduation, the higher the likelihood a cardiac patient would die in that doctor's care in the hospital.

Your doctor trained at an American medical school. A study of cardiac patients in Pennsylvania found that those who were managed by foreign-born and foreign-trained doctors were less likely to die than those who studied in U.S. medical schools. The author of the study speculated that the difference was the result of primary care in the U.S. becoming less attractive to American medical school grads, and thus less competitive. By comparison, the foreign international medical school grads who manage to jump through the hoops required to come and practice in the U.S. are among the highest achievers worldwide.

WHAT'S EATING YOU?

While it sounds like something out of science fiction or an urban legend, the terrifying flesh-eating virus is quite real. Also known as *necrotizing fasciitis*, it was first discovered in the nineteenth century, but it's likely centuries older than that. The disease wasn't officially documented until 1952.

What makes necrotizing fasciitis so frightening is the rate at which it relentlessly eradicates human tissue. But don't worry, it doesn't really "eat" skin and muscle. It actually destroys them by releasing incredibly aggressive bacterial toxins. (Feel better?)

The disease tends to impact people with drug or alcohol problems or those with diabetes or an otherwise weakened constitution. Necrotizing fasciitis typically enters the body via an open wound. Victims report that the first sign of trouble is soreness not unlike that of a pulled muscle. This is followed by fever, skin inflammation, and increased heart rate. Within mere hours, the area around the wound becomes discolored and swollen; and often large blisters develop.

Most victims also experience severe diarrhea and vomiting–oh, and *crepitus*, a popping noise or strange sensation caused by air pockets that develop under the skin while the disease begins to destroy the flesh of its human host. One more icky detail: The infection zone emits a milky fluid that resembles dishwater.

If left untreated, the disease can consume an astonishing three centimeters of tissue per hour. Those foolish enough not to seek immediate medical attention face a 75 percent mortality rate, in addition to almost guaranteed disfigurement. Treatments include powerful antibiotics and surgery to remove the infected flesh. There is no known cure.

Because it's so rare, it's also hard to get, so that's good. But protect yourself against flesh-eating disease the same way you guard against other sicknesses: wash your hands, take care of cuts, and stay away from coughing people.

Bonus: Jeff Hannemann, a guitarist with the heavy metal band Slayer, contracted the flesh-eating disease in 2011. That's pretty metal—as is the fact that he survived. Two years later, however, he died from liver failure, brought on by a weakened immune system.

+ + +

SWITCHEROO

In 2006 a woman unnamed in reports underwent a hysterectomy in Kentucky. The woman's uterus was removed…and replaced with a surgical sponge. It wasn't discovered for six months, at which time it was removed, along with part of her small intestine (which had become infected because of the sponge). A jury awarded her $2.5 million in damages.

WIDE AWAKE AND CUT WIDE OPEN

Imagine being in excruciating pain but unable to move, speak, or do anything to alert anyone else about your condition. Should this happen to you, you're either sitting through a grade-school production of Wagner's *Ring* Cycle or you're awake while under anesthetic during surgery.

Sarah Newton experienced one of the worst cases of waking up under the knife. In 2011 she underwent surgery to drain brain fluid out of her stomach and spine, which accumulated due to a condition called *intracranial hypertension*. She regained consciousness during the last hour of her operation. "I could feel them cutting my stomach open," she said. "I could hear them talking, but I could not move at all. I was trying to scream. I could feel every stitch going in. I counted all the stitches. Now, it's infinite counting in my nightmares."

Carol Weiher was having her right eyeball removed in 1998 when she heard the doctor asking his assistant to "cut deeper, pull harder." There was no pain from the actual incisions, but the injections of a paralytic drug during the operation "felt like ignited fuel."

"I was doing a combination of praying and pleading and cursing and screaming, but I knew that there was nothing that was working," Weiher told CNN. "I thought, well, maybe I've been wrong about my life, and I'm in hell."

Know that there is a bright side. A brain-wave monitor can now be used to successfully prevent such horrific experiences from occurring. But as this technology costs money, it's only utilized in 17 percent of hospitals worldwide.

The good news is that this happens to a mere 1 percent of surgical patients in any given year. But, hey, go ahead and schedule that unnecessary nose job! Everything will *probably* be just fine.

✚ ✚ ✚

YOU GOTTA HAVE HEART

In August 2006, 55-year-old Louis Selo of London died while on vacation in Ireland. His body was examined at Beaumont Hospital in Dublin, where it was determined that Selo had died of a massive heart attack. The corpse was sent home to England, where another autopsy was performed (a second autopsy is customarily done when English citizens die out of the country).

That operation went a bit differently: When the English doctors opened up Selo's chest, they discovered an extra heart and two extra lungs in a plastic bag inside him. An inquiry revealed that they were from an organ donor at the Irish hospital. Those organs were returned to the family of the donor, and an investigation to find out how they ended up in Mr. Selo was begun immediately.

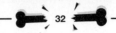

THROWING IN THE TOWEL

An *aortic aneurysm* is a bulging of a section of the aorta, the body's primary artery system. This bulge, which most commonly occurs in the part of the aorta that runs through the abdomen, can burst, which is why 59-year-old William Barlow reported for surgery in 2000 at a Veterans Administration hospital in Florida.

The aortic aneurysm was fixed, but Barlow kept getting sicker. A week after the surgery, he registered a fever of 105 degrees and had developed sepsis, an infection of the blood that can lead to organ failure and death. A CT scan revealed that there was a foreign object in his abdomen, but it was unclear what.

It wasn't until the second surgery, in early 2001, that doctors found what the previous doctors had left inside Barlow: a 16-by-28-inch cotton surgical towel. That's as big as a bath towel, only it's thinner, so instead of sitting there in a huge lump, it was able to wrap itself around Barlow's guts.

Barlow sued the VA. Attorneys for the organization admitted the mistake, and offered Barlow $100,000, arguing that his overall poor health (he'd also had a cancerous kidney removed) and obesity were factors in his development of sepsis, because, by this logic, a gigantic towel lodged in his gut shouldn't have been so serious. Barlow refused the offer and took the case to trial. There, a judge awarded him $450,000.

A HAND UP, NOT A HAND OUT

After losing his right hand in what was reportedly an industrial accident in 1998, Clint Hallam of New Zealand had a few options: have no hand, have a hook hand like a pirate, or let a team of microsurgeons in France transplant the forearm of a dead guy.

Hallam went with the surgery, largely because it would be free, as would a lifetime supply of anti-rejection drugs; it was *that* experimental. Hallam merely had to endure months of rigorous psychological evaluation to determine whether he was emotionally capable of living with another man's hand attached to his body.

The tests didn't reveal one major bit of information: Hallam hadn't lost the hand in an industrial accident—he'd lost it in prison, when he was goofing around with a chainsaw (as one does). He also turned out to be spectacularly unsuited for the surgery. Hallam's new hand progressed to the point that he could write with it, hold a fork, and feel pain. But then he went off his anti-rejection drugs and stopped going in for checkups.

Hallam's body ultimately rejected the new hand, making it shrivel up and atrophy, and in 2001 he had to have it surgically removed. (The second surgery wasn't free: Hallam had to pay $4,000.)

SIDE EFFECTS MAY INCLUDE...

Evil eyes
Latisse is a by-prescription cosmetic medication that promises longer eyelashes. But that's not all it delivers. In addition to minor expected side effects such as redness and itchiness, some patients have suffered from hyperpigmentation: dark purple rings around their eyes. "Raccoon eyes" isn't a great or desired look, particularly for those who only wanted luscious lashes. In rare cases, Latisse can even change the very color of the eyes. According to the manufacturer, these side effects "may be reversible."

Amnesia
A class of cholesterol drugs called statins have been known to cause memory loss. The most extreme case was Duane Graveline, a former astronaut who took Lipitor and promptly forgot large swaths of his entire life after high school, including a lot of his time as an astronaut. But if you're thinking of stopping your medication, forget it. Most doctors agree the benefits outweigh the risks. (And memory loss is typically temporary.)

Sensory loss
The high-blood-pressure medication Vasotec may save you from congestive heart failure. It may also take away your senses of sight, sound, taste, and smell, though usually not all at once. The most

common of these side effects are *anosmia* (loss of smell) and *tinnitus* (an overpowering ringing in your ears). The maker of Vasotec describes these side effects as "minor" (at least that's what we think we heard).

Multicolored urine

If you've ever changed a newborn's diaper, you're familiar with the rainbow of colors possible in an infant's feces. But did you know that certain drugs can make your urine change color? If you want purple pee, try phenolphthalein, a laxative that may also cause cancer. Elavil, an antidepressant, gives you green urine. The diuretic Dyrenium makes it blue.

Larger breasts...in men

Some balding men choose to stimulate their manhood by taking prescription hair-growth medication. This sometimes backfires when finasteride (the active ingredient in the oral hair-restoration drug Propecia) causes a rare condition called gynecomastia. That's doc talk for male breast enlargement. But it's worse than a couple of unwanted sweater kittens…they often lactate, too.

COMA, NO COMA, COMA?

In 1983, a Belgian man named Rom Houben was in a devastating car accident. Houben was left quadriplegic and with serious brain injuries that left him in a coma. Using the Glasgow Coma Scale, a method of measuring brain activity in coma patients or those in an otherwise vegetative state, doctors concluded that Houben's brain was minimally functioning.

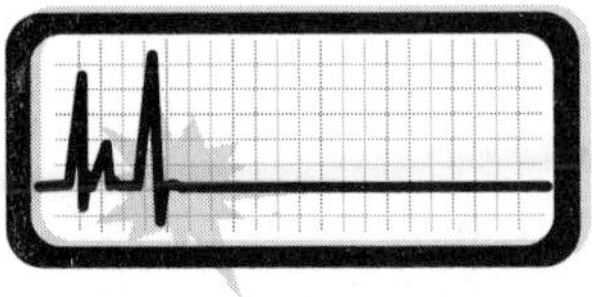

Or so they thought. In 2006, more than 20 years after Houben's accident, University of Liege neurologist Steven Laureys performed more modern tests on Houben that supplanted the Glasgow Coma Scale. Laureys was astonished to discover that Houben's brain was functioning normally. All that time, Houben wasn't really in a coma, or even unconscious–he was well aware of his surroundings, suffering from a horrifying condition called "locked-in syndrome." First identified in 1966, it describes patients who are almost completely paralyzed with the exception of their eyes. The past 23 years of Houben's life had evidently been a living nightmare. He had been able to observe the world around him but had no ability to tell his doctors about it. His body had become a prison.

With the aid of a facilitator who helped him use a specially wired keyboard, Houben was able to reacquaint himself with his friends and family, and announced that he was going to write a book about his experiences. Skeptics, meanwhile, remained unconvinced and theorized that this was all an unintentional hoax perpetuated by his naïve facilitator and overly optimistic doctors.

The skeptics were right. Another round of tests conducted in 2010 determined that Houben was unable to answer simple one-word questions…if his facilitator left the room. Dr. Laureys, in addition to medical experts, the media, and Houben's family, had all been duped.

Houben isn't the first case of this phenomenon. Facilitated communication, used to help coma victims and people with severe autism communicate, has been widely debunked, in part because of the Houben case. Much like teenagers playing with a Ouija board, facilitators tend to subconsciously communicate on behalf of their patients. They don't realize what they're doing—Laureys hadn't meant to fool anyone. It was merely wishful thinking on the part of a medical community that so desperately wanted the story to be true.

+ + +

WHERE DO BROKEN HEARTS GO?

In 1995, a 33-year-old South Carolina man shot himself, and his heart was transplanted into 56-year-old Sonny Sugarman. The new heart took care of Sugarman's congestive heart failure, but 13 years later, Sugarman also shot himself. Even weirder: the heart donor's widowed wife married Sugarman.

ME SECTION

In 2002 Inés Ramírez of remote Rio Talea, Mexico, went into labor. It had been a stressful pregnancy, in part because she'd lost her last child during childbirth. And once again, Ramírez felt that something wasn't right. Even worse was that she was 50 miles from the nearest midwife and had no phone, electricity, or running water. After 12 hours of increasingly difficult labor, Ramírez decided to do something–deliver the baby herself, and get it over with.

First, she drank a few shots of liquor as a makeshift anesthetic. Then she grabbed a sharp kitchen knife and made a cut low on her belly. Maybe the knife wasn't that sharp, after all, because she had to keep cutting, and cutting, and *cutting*, for an hour, until finally she reached her womb.

The rest was easy: She bent down, reached into her womb, and pulled out a baby boy. Ramírez sent one of her sons for help, while she got down to the business of passing out. Some hours later, a local health aide arrived and, after getting over his shock, stitched up Ms. Ramírez's belly–using ordinary needle and thread–and then drove her to a hospital in the city of Oaxaca.

Both the mother and child survived. It is the only known case in history of a woman successfully performing a cesarean section on herself.

AN IRONING IRONY

People have long shown a willingness to do whatever they can to look like their favorite celebrities. Remember all those women with Jennifer Aniston hairdos in the '90s?

That was all in good fun, but 2013 marks the year celebrity copycat-ism went too far. That's when movie star George Clooney mentioned in an interview that as he had to regularly have his scrotum "ironed" to remove the wrinkles. It should be noted that scrotum wrinkling was not a service offered by cosmeticians or cosmetic surgeons at the time. Clooney made it up. He was *joking*. However, so many men requested the service that a California spa began offering a "Male Laser Lift. The $600 procedure uses lasers to correct discoloration and remove wrinkles on the scrotum. Yes, this procedure sounds really strange and unnecessary, but not any more so than Clooney's *Batman & Robin*.

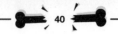

THE FACE MELTER

Protozoan parasites are single-cell organisms too monstrous to be classified as bacteria. (It's more complicated than that, but if we were biologists, we wouldn't be writing trivia books.) Typically spread by insects, the deadliest of these diseases is malaria. But the most gruesome is *leishmaniasis*–it kills you by eating your face.

Leishmaniasis is essentially microscopic flesh-eating bugs, transmitted by equally disgusting sand fleas. And when these tiny desert insects decide to use your skin as an oasis, bad things happen. The most common strain causes horrific leprosy-like lesions that leave lifelong scars. But the most virulent target your nose and mouth, often devouring them completely. Oh, they also cause organ failure and death.

Medical historians have found references to leishmaniasis going back to 2500 BC. And while we've stopped fighting leishmaniasis by eating camel dung and burning witches, today's cures are almost as bad as the disease itself. Some patients remain nauseous and immobile for years. The worst part is that the infection can incubate for just as long before erupting. So if you've visited South America or the Middle East in the past few years, you may have brought back a bonus souvenir without even knowing it.

If your face explodes in bloody open sores, see your doctor.

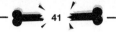

WHAT'S YOUR EMERGENCY?

While playing racquetball with friends at the Nova Community Center in Ormand Beach, Florida, in 2013, Bob Hill suffered a heart attack. A friend called 911 and gave the correct cross streets, but mistakenly said they were at the Ormand Rec Center–not the Nova Community Center. A dispatch trainee then looked up the address of the Ormand Rec Center (despite having been given the correct address where Hill actually was) and sent paramedics there. Ten minutes passed before the trainee and the caller realized the mistake. Between the time of the call and the time an ambulance finally arrived at the correct location to treat Hill, he was dead.

Throughout, the trainee was supposed to be supervised by a veteran dispatcher, 28-year-old Shauna Justice. Volusia County, Florida, videotapes all of its 911 activity, and tapes show that instead of supervising the trainee, Justice spent the time playing on her cell phone. Justice was given a five-day suspension, and her superiors apologized publicly.

Three days into her suspension, Justice was visited at home by a local TV news reporter. Justice stormed out of her house and threatened the reporter with a gun. For that, she was charged with aggravated assault.

GETTING THEIR GOAT

For men with bedroom-performance issues, there's always been the promise of a magical cure, from witch doctors to medicine shows to Viagra. One notable cure purveyor was Dr. John R. Brinkley, who promised men newfound virility via surgically implanted goat testicles.

A farmer with "no lead in his pencil" came to him seeking help. Brinkley joked that what the man needed were the glands of a frisky billy goat. The farmer begged him for just such an operation, and the doctor (who had a degree from Kansas City's finest diploma mill) obliged. The farmer's wife went on to give birth to a son, which they named "Billy," and the promotional blitz that followed sent thousands of men shuffling to Brinkley's door.

Brinkley would cut open a man's scrotum and insert plugs harvested from goat glands into the testicles. Often, patient's bodies would reject the foreign material; 43 of Brinkley's patients reportedly died. In addition to the risks of the procedure, patients complained of a unsanitary surgical environment and Brinkley sometimes operating while drunk. Still, this was not a bad rate of return for a surgery performed more than 16,000 times.

RING'S FINGER

Dr. David C. Ring, a Massachusetts General Hospital orthopedic surgeon, was having a terrible, horrible, no good, very bad day. First, he'd performed six operations on that 2010 day, far more than usual. One of them hadn't gone well. A patient who'd had a carpal tunnel release surgery responded poorly to the anesthetic–the shot left her hands in extreme pain and had also left her agitated and panicky. Ring unsuccessfully tried to calm her down.

A number of factors led Dr. Ring to perform the wrong operation on his next patient. The 65-year-old woman was supposed to have surgery to correct her painful, permanently bent finger, commonly called a "trigger-release" operation. A last-minute change in the operating room meant that the nurse in charge wasn't around for a pre-op assessment. And while the patient's finger had been marked as a fail-safe, the ink washed off when the patient's hands were cleaned just before the surgery. Distracted by the previous carpal tunnel release, Dr. Ring performed a carpal tunnel release on the patient, not a trigger release.

Only when he was reviewing his reports at the end of the day did Dr. Ring notice his error. He immediately performed the correct operation; a few weeks later, he went public with his story and held a conference about how to prevent wrong-site surgery.

TATTOO YOU

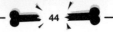

There are a lot of options available to surgeons who want to make a positive impression on their patients after the fact. A follow-up phone call is always appreciated. A postcard is a bit old-fashioned, but still classy. Slapping a tattoo on the patient's body while they're zonked out? Not so much.

And yet that's exactly what Dr. Steven Kirshner was sued for in July 2008. Specifically, Dr. Kirshner was accused of rubbing a temporary rose tattoo on a patient's belly, below her panty line, after surgery. That's weird enough, but it crosses the line into creepy when you realize that the patient was lying on her stomach for the surgery, which means he flipped the patient over, while she was unconscious, just to apply the tattoo.

Dr. Kirshner admitted to placing the tattoo but said he did so to help the patient feel better. Because nothing lifts a person's spirits after surgery more than knowing that their doctor feels free to leave stuff on their body while they're naked and unconscious.

BRAND STRATEGY

Surgery is bad enough, but to find out that your doctor used a cauterizing tool to write your name on the organ he just removed? Insult to injury.

Ingrid Paulicivic underwent a hysterectomy in 2009. After the surgery, she experienced unexpected burns on her legs and complained of pain on a follow-up visit to the surgeon, Dr. Red Alinsod. Alinsod produced digital photos of the surgery and shared those with the patient. Upon examining the pics, Paulicivic discovered that Alinsod had taken time after her surgery to write "Ingrid" in inch-high letters across the surgical site.

Alinsod told *The Smoking Gun* that the branding was intended as a "gesture of friendship," although the patient claimed she hadn't met Alinsod till their initial consult. He explained he wrote the name on the uterus so that he wouldn't confuse it with others, although he also admitted that a simple note on a sterile towel or tongue depressor usually does the trick. That also raises the question of how many uteruses he leaves lying around his operating room on an average day that he can't tell them apart.

Dr. Alinsod is not even the first surgeon to do this. In 2003 Dr. James Guiler was sued by a group of female patients for etching the initials of his alma mater, "UK" (for the University of Kentucky), onto their uteruses during hysterectomies.

EVERYDAY HEALTH MYTHS, DEBUNKED

You should drink eight glasses of water every day. Water is important for health, but experts say that eight glasses is a bit much. Most people get plenty of hydration from the water contained within the food and drinks they consume. The best way to tell if you're getting enough? If your urine looks too yellow, you need more water.

Echinacea prevents colds. Studies show that, while this popular herbal remedy improves white blood cell counts and can boost one's immune system, it doesn't minimize the duration or severity of an average case of the sniffles, let alone prevent one. A 2005 study by the *New England Journal of Medicine* found that the herb is no more effective than a placebo.

An apple a day keeps the doctor away. Unless you catch the plague. Or the flu. Or a cold. While studies show that eating one every day can reduce your chances of a heart attack by 32 percent (they're high in fiber) and improve your immune system a bit (they've got vitamins), no amount of apples will keep you perfectly healthy. They also consistently fall on the USDA's top 10 list of the most contaminated fruits–they easily absorb pesticides.

Eating carrots improves your eyesight. Carrots are full of beta-carotene (vitamin A) and eating them promotes excellent eye health. That doesn't mean that they'll magically improve your vision. So where did this myth come from? During the London Blitz in World War II, the British Royal Air Force was able to repel the Nazis' relentless aerial bombardment in part due to a new form of radar technology that they were eager to keep under wraps. When the British press asked the RAF how their pilots were able to shoot down so many German planes in the dark, they told reporters that pilots were eating tons of carrots to boost their eyesight. This shrewd explanation also encouraged the British public to eat more of them, since it was one of the few fruits and veggies that weren't being rationed.

If you pick dropped food off the floor within five seconds, you can still eat it and not get sick. Also known as "the five-second rule," this bit of advice may have originated with Genghis Khan. Supposedly, the emperor once ordered his followers not to eat food that had been sitting on the ground for over 12 hours. Of course, Khan's recommended timing was steadily whittled down over the years, but a 2007 study argues that we should all adopt a "zero second rule." Conducted by Clemson University food scientist Paul Dawson, the study proved that salmonella can bounce onto fallen food in less than a second.

IT'S A RECORD!

Worst kidney blockage. In June 1999, a 35-year-old man checked into a Saudi Arabian hospital with a bad case of *hydronephrosis*—an enlarged kidney due to an obstruction in urine flow. Doctors removed 5.8 gallons of urine from the kidney (and then, a few weeks later, they removed the kidney, too).

Most surgeries. William McIlroy of Great Britain had been diagnosed with Munchausen syndrome, a psychological condition that makes people fake medical problems because they crave attention. McIlroy talked the talk, though, because between 1929 and 1979, he underwent an amazing and unnecessary 400 operations at 100 different UK hospitals using 22 aliases.

Largest cancerous tumor. In 2010 doctors in Argentina removed an 8.7-pound growth from the uterus of a 54-year-old woman. They tested it, and it was a malignant tumor. That's roughly the same weight as a large newborn baby.

Largest noncancerous tumor. In 1991 doctors at Stanford University Medical Center operated on the abdomen of a 34-year-old woman and, six hours later, pulled out a 303-pound, 37-inch-diameter benign tumor. (The woman, unnamed in reports, was unable to have the tumor removed any earlier due to severe agoraphobia.)

Highest blood sugar level. For a normal, healthy person, a blood sugar level runs about 90 mg/dl. Diabetics' levels run a little higher. In May 2008, seven-year-old Michael Buonocore checked into a Pennsylvania emergency room with a reading of 26,656. He survived, but was diagnosed with diabetes.

Largest kidney stone. A kidney stone considered "large" is about the size of a golf ball. The one doctors removed from a Hungarian man named Sandor Sarkadi in 2009 was as big around as a coconut and weighed 2.48 pounds.

Most kidney stones surgically removed. Urologist Dr. Ashish Rawandale-Patil removed 172,155 kidney stones, varying in size from 1 mm to 2.5 cm in diameter, from just one of Dhanraj Wadile's kidneys in 2010. (The previous record was a paltry 14,098 stones.) "The surgery was complicated due to the number of kidney stones," Dr. Rawandale-Patil deadpanned to reporters.

Most kidney stones passed naturally (and painfully). Canadian Donald Winfield will never forget August 2006, for that is the month that he naturally passed 5,704 kidney stones.

TOO MUCH CHEMO

Cancer is the greatest and deadliest foe of the human race. It attacks people in all walks of life—and it can strike without warning or reason on any part of the body. The disease is so ravaging and has touched so many lives that it's truly a triumphant moment when a fellow human, helped by the miracles of modern-day science, can fight cancer into remission, and go on to live cancer-free. Betsy Lehman was one of those fighters. That's why her story is so alarming and sad.

In December 1994, Lehman underwent what doctors at the Dana-Farber Cancer Institute in Boston believed to be her final round of chemotherapy for advanced breast cancer. A doctor was supposed to instruct Lehman's medical team to administer 1,630 mg of the chemotherapy drug Cytoxan once a day for four days. Instead, Lehman was given four times the daily amount every day for four days.

Lehman, ironically a health reporter for the *Boston Globe*, began to vomit intensely and told the doctors that she felt something had gone very wrong. The medical staff did not suspect overdose and believed her symptoms were reactions to chemotherapy, even ignoring tests that indicated she had heart damage (another side effect of chemo). Unfortunately, Lehman's heart stopped.

An autopsy revealed that Lehman, the mother of a seven-year-old and a three-year-old, was cancer-free.

MY THROAT IS ON FIRE

We've all had a cold, the flu, or strep throat, all of which can leave our throats feeling raw and burning. But that's not literally true—merely an approximation of how bad the pain feels. This is not what happened to Becky Anderson. In February 2012, the 55-year-old checked into Central Washington Hospital for an elective surgery: laser removal of nondangerous but annoying polyps from her larynx.

While she was under anesthesia, however, her breathing tube ruptured…and then it improbably burst into flame. It instantly and literally burned Anderson's throat. She had to have several more surgeries to correct the damage done by the accident. In the middle of what would ultimately be a three-month hospital stay to treat her rare case of internal burns, she decided to sue her doctors and Central Washington Hospital.

Anderson was awarded $30 million from the medical facilities and her doctors. Another lawsuit was dismissed, against medical device manufacturer Medtronic, maker of the air tube. Anderson's lawyers argued that the machine lacked fail-safes to prevent the oxygen from exploding, although Anderson (and the jury) put most of the blame on her doctors, who did not use regular air in her breathing tube but pure oxygen, which is far more flammable.

PUERPERAL PROSE

In the 1840s, Ignaz Semmelweiss was the assistant to the director of the maternity clinic at Vienna General Hospital in Austria. Vienna General was a teaching hospital, which meant young doctors spent many hours each day performing autopsies and then delivering babies, as both are educational.

Vienna General was also a prominent breeding ground for puerperal fever. Also known as "childbed fever," it's a lethal infection that strikes women immediately following childbirth. When the body is weak after giving birth, the infection easily takes hold, usually entering through the woman's exposed genitals. A fever of more than 100 degrees results, and if not treated, it can kill a woman within 10 days. At Vienna General, 18 percent of new mothers were dying of puerperal fever. But, Semmelweiss noticed, only 1 percent of new mothers in a nearby midwifery were succumbing to the infection.

Semmelweiss analyzed hospital data and found that the mothers who had contracted puerperal fever had had their babies delivered by doctors reporting immediately after autopsy duty. He concluded that the doctors were carrying the pathogen from the corpses directly to the vulnerable new mothers—an early "aha" moment of what Joseph Lister and Louis Pasteur would call, later in the nineteenth century, "germ theory."

Semmelweiss presented his findings to his colleagues. Although this was a teaching hospital, these doctors refused to learn. In fact, many were offended that Semmelweiss would accuse them of being unclean. He wasn't–he just thought that handwashing was a simple and effective way to cut down on the transmission of puerperal fever. What did they think was causing the outbreak of puerperal fever? Cut flowers on patients' bedside tables.

Coming to Semmelweiss's side was prominent British doctor and writer Oliver Wendell Holmes, who published an article called "The Contagiousness of Puerperal Fever," arguing in favor of Semmelweiss's theory. Semmelweiss begged doctors delivering babies to wash their hands with a chlorinated lime solution and to change their clothes after handling corpses. They refused, so he took to barricading the maternity ward from anyone who didn't comply.

By the 1860s, Semmelweiss's procedures had finally taken hold at Vienna General. As a result, childbirth mortality dropped from 18 percent to just 2 percent. Was Semmelweiss lauded by the medical community for his efforts? Hardly. In 1865, Semmelweiss was committed to a mental institution. Colleagues thought he was going mad, but historians now believe he was showing early signs of the yet-to-be identified Alzheimer's disease. At the mental institution he was viciously beaten by guards and died at age 47, just two weeks after he had been committed.

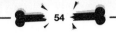

A SHOT FROM THE DARK

In 2007 *Playboy* playmate, MTV personality, and e-cigarette spokeswoman Jenny McCarthy appeared on *The Oprah Winfrey Show*, one of the most influential shows on television. McCarthy, who has no medical training, was there to reveal the shocking connection between the widely administered MMR vaccine (that's "mumps, measles, rubella") and autism.

McCarthy cited the research of Andrew Wakefield, a British doctor who had published a study illustrating a connection between children who had been vaccinated (as the vast majority of American children are), and those who were later diagnosed with autism. Almost overnight, the vaccines that had spared millions of children from disease were being called into question. Thousands of parents quickly decided to not vaccinate their children.

One problem: There is no connection between MMR and autism. *Sunday Times* journalist Brian Deer published extensive proof that Wakefield stood to profit significantly from discrediting the MMR vaccine–he had his own "alternate," supposedly non-autism-causing, vaccine about to come to market.

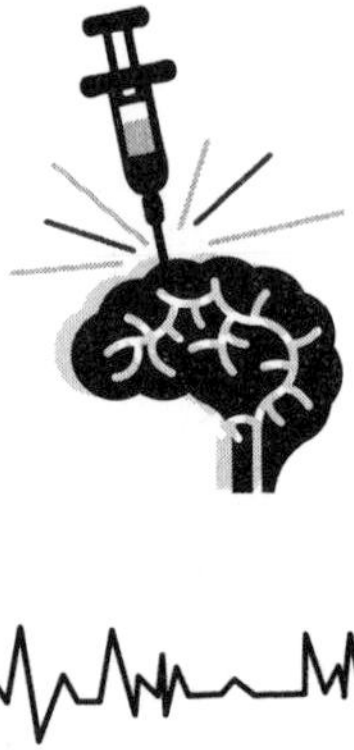

Do not underestimate the power of Oprah: By 2009 record outbreaks of measles were being reported in the UK, Canada, Australia, and the United States.

THE MAN WITH THE 160-POUND SCROTUM

Having big *cojones* is a good thing only in the metaphorical sense. To literally have extremely large testicles is a serious medical problem that few men would have the metaphorical cojones to handle. Such was life for Las Vegas resident Wesley Warren Jr., who made national headlines in 2008 when an accidental trauma to his testicles caused his scrotum to swell to the size of a soccer ball. Eventually his scrotum, growing at a rate of three pounds per month, exceeded 160 pounds.

Doctors told Warren they could help him, but only for a price that would make his grossly enlarged scrotum seem tiny in comparison. So as anyone with a highly visible medical problem would do, he turned to Howard Stern for help. But even going on Stern's show didn't help him raise enough money for corrective surgery. Warren also turned down an offer from Dr. Oz to perform the surgery for free.

"HIS SCROTUM, GROWING AT A RATE OF THREE POUNDS PER MONTH, EXCEEDED 160 POUNDS."

Finally, in April 2013, Warren was successfully operated on by a team of four surgeons. His story was made into a documentary film shown the world over, which is just nuts.

DOCTORED DOCTORATES

For as long as there have been doctors, there have been phony doctors. A banner year for bad medicine was 1984—federal investigators arrested more than 100 fraudulent physicians in New York alone. Worse than individual decoy doctors is the unethical infrastructure that supports them: fake degrees from fake schools with fake accreditation. Minting counterfeit quacks has become its own industry, one so sophisticated you might even say counterfeiters have it down to a science. (Our particular pretend PhD is in punnery.)

With the rise of the Internet, med schools that are neither medical nor schools are becoming more and more commonplace. If you see diplomas from any of these institutions on your doctor's wall, run. (Unless that doctor just prescribed running, in which case, don't—these fake doctors are not to be trusted.)

University of Health Sciences, Antigua. UHS Antigua has been awarding fake MDs for nearly 40 years. Since this for-profit school is located in a Caribbean paradise, it's odd how little time most students spend on campus. Probably because it only takes eight weeks of classes to earn a four-year medical degree. What efficiency! The downside is graduates will be banned from legally working in California, Texas, and most other states.

Stewart University International School of Medicine. Stewart is like UHS Antigua but with one major distinction: It's stateside. Located a few physical, but infinite philosophical miles from Stanford University, Stewart describes itself as "the #1 leader in U.S. medical education." What are the admissions standards for this esteemed California institution? No college degree required, no letters of recommendation needed; there isn't even a minimum application age. So you could be an eight-year-old boy with a federal murder warrant and no grade school diploma and you'd have a shot at Stewart U, provided you're willing to pay the $950 nonrefundable "seat reservation fee," of course.

Saint Luke School of Medicine, Liberia. The prize for most madcap, mysterious diploma factory goes to this African sham school. Since it opened in 1998, St. Luke's remained undistinguished among the unseemly. Then the Liberian government made a shocking announcement: The school does not exist. Despite graduating (though not actually educating) thousands, regulators claimed they couldn't locate any campus or track down any staff. St. Luke's founder insisted he was simply being slandered for failing to bribe Liberian officials, then promptly fled the country. That was back in 2005. Thankfully, St. Luke's is still up and running online, where you can get a medical degree in "Independent Study."

THE WORLD'S WORST DIARRHEA

Diarrhea. It's pretty bad, but some kinds are even worse than others. Some say the worst variety is "traveler's diarrhea," also known as "Montezuma's revenge," acquired via travel in foreign lands where a person isn't used to the local germs and so falls ill. Most victims are back on their feet after a few hours, or a day or two of unpleasantness. This is a cakewalk compared to Brainerd diarrhea.

A typical case of Brainerd diarrhea tends to begin, as diarrhea does, abruptly. Victims are hit with a sudden blast of watery and explosive diarrhea, but that's just the beginning. The condition can last for not just hours, not just days, but *weeks.* The first documented case occurred in 1983 in Brainerd, Minnesota, hence the name. (We're sure the city has been trying to shake off the affiliation ever since.)

According to the Centers for Disease Control and Prevention, each day victims experience 10 to 20 episodes of watery bowel movements "characterized by urgency." Additional symptoms include gas, cramps, fatigue, nausea, and fever. But there's a bonus: The vast majority of people who contract Brainerd diarrhea tend to lose a few pounds.

The average case lasts four weeks, but at least a few have dragged on for years—one poor soul dealt with Brainerd diarrhea for an astounding three years.

Researchers have yet to discover the specific cause, but they believe the condition can be transmitted through the consumption of raw milk or untreated water. Amazingly enough, there are no documented cases of the condition ever killing anyone.

While no antibiotic on the planet has been found capable of curing Brainerd diarrhea, the condition is, thankfully, rare. The incident in 1983 that gave the sickness its name remains its worst outbreak to date, with 122 victims. Since then, there have been only six additional outbreaks, the largest of which occurred in Fannin County, Texas, in 1996, in which 117 people got sick due to contaminated water. Roughly half of the victims fell ill after eating tomatoes and drinking tap water at a local restaurant.

So, you know, wash your hands, and maybe order bottled water if you're ever in Brainerd or Fannin County.

✚ ✚ ✚

BLOOD SIMPLE

In 1665, English surgeon Richard Lower attempted one of the first modern-day blood transfusions. He practiced sending blood between two dogs, fashioning extremely thing transfusion tubes out of feather quills. The dogs survived, so Lower moved on to transfuse lamb blood into a human. The man died…which lead to the end of transfusion research until the 1830s.

SPONGEBOB SPINEBACK

Who lives in a spine after not being removed?

SpongeBob SpineBack!

Absorbent and yellow and toxic was he.

SpongeBob SpineBack!

Falton, Maryland, resident John P. Freel began to notice extreme discomfort in his back after being discharged from the Maryland Spine Center for a related surgery. He chalked it up to normal postsurgical aches and pains. But 17 days after the surgery, Freel received a phone call from the attending surgeon, Dr. Spiros Antoniades. The source of his pain wasn't normal: Antoniades admitted that he had forgotten to remove a surgical sponge before closing Freel's incision.

Even after admitting his error, Dr. Antoniades tried to persuade his patient that it wasn't necessary to remove the foreign object and that observation would be just fine for the time being. Freel's body, on the other hand, disagreed. Freel suffered from a sponge-related staph infection and had to have surrounding fibrous tissue removed, along with the sponge. Dr. Antoniades would later be sued by Freel for medical negligence.

THE SURGERY WAS A SUCCESS, BUT WE TOOK A LITTLE SOMETHING EXTRA

When 67-year-old Hurshell Ralls awoke after surgery, his wife was at the bedside holding his hand. She told him she had good news: The doctors had removed all the cancer from his bladder. But there was some bad news: The doctors had also removed his penis and testicles.

"I was one mad dude," Ralls told reporters after the surgery—and with good reason. According to Ralls, doctors had never suggested the possibility of removing his tackle. And to add insult to castration, there was no cancer in Ralls's penis. Doctors made the decision to neuter during surgery and neglected to conduct a tissue sample. Cells taken from Ralls's former glory later tested negative for penile cancer.

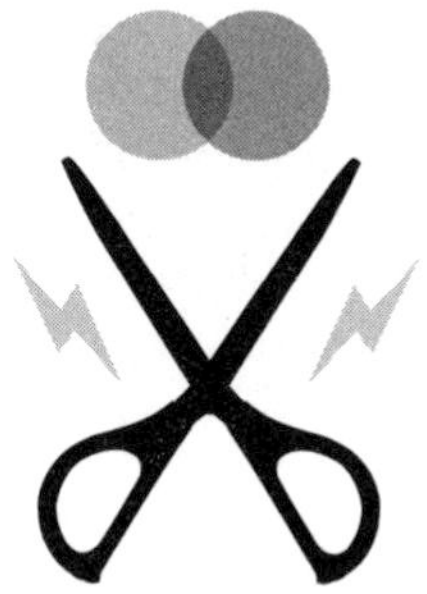

A settlement was reached in Ralls's civil suit after only two days of trial for an undisclosed amount. But his story lives on for men everywhere as a horrifying final thought before the anesthetic kicks in.

STONE COLD CRAZY

In 1651 Jan de Doot, an Amsterdam blacksmith, began having terrible pains in his groin. He could feel something hard through his skin–it was a bladder stone. It was diagnosed as such by Dr. Nicolaes Tulp, mayor of Amsterdam and one of the most renowned surgeons of the era. De Doot didn't trust doctors…or at least not enough to let one operate on him. He'd given himself no other option but to remove that stone himself.

With only his brother (who also wasn't a doctor) standing by in case something went wrong, de Doot used a small, sharp knife to cut through his perineum (the floor of the crotch, or the area of skin between the scrotum and the rectum), where he could feel the stone. To get the stone out was more difficult, and he had to stick two fingers into the wound on either side to remove it with leveraged force. It finally popped out of hiding, literally, with an explosive noise and tearing of the bladder. The stone was the size of a chicken egg. When the operation was completed, de Doot had his brother summon a doctor's assistant to stitch up his wound. De Doot recovered nicely.

After the surgery, he sat for a painting by Flemish artist Carel van Savoyen. In it, de Doot is depicted holding a knife in one hand, and in the other he's holding up an egg-shaped object–the stone he cut from his own body.

STONE MAN DISEASE

F*ibrodysplasia ossificans progressiva,* sometimes called "stone man disease," causes the fibrous connective tissue of the body, including the tissue that makes up muscles and ligaments, to heal itself by ossifying. That is, it turns into bone.

This genetic disease often goes undiagnosed for the first few years of a child's life, though individuals with the disease are born with malformed big toes. Generally it first affects the neck and shoulders, usually before the age of 10. The bone growth causes loss of mobility in the joints, and eventually can cause problems with breathing (bone growth inhibits the movement of the rib cage) as well as problems eating and speaking.

The disease is incredibly rare, with only one case in every two million people and only a couple hundred confirmed cases in history. There are currently no available treatments, not even surgery. The bone growth is progressive, and surgical treatment actually worsens the disease, since removing the bone growth through surgery causes more bone growth at the surgery site. Flare-ups, with swelling followed by bone growth, can be caused by an injury, such as a fall, or by viral illnesses, such as the flu. Sufferers rarely live past 40.

HE AIN'T HEAVY, HE'S MY BROTHER

Igor Namyatov first went to a doctor for back pain when he was 15 years old. After a cursory medical exam, his doctor told him that the source of his pain was a "fatty growth" in his back, but that it was harmless and it didn't need to be removed. Namyatov agreed, because the pain went away.

The back pain returned 20 years later. This time, doctors told Namyatov that the pain wasn't from a fatty growth–it was a tumor. A benign tumor, but a massive tumor nonetheless. Namyatov had surgery, and that's when doctors discovered that teenage Namyatov's doctor had been right after all–well, sort of. It was a lump of fatty tissue all right, but it had hands. And legs. It was Namyatov's malformed, unborn twin brother.

In what is a rare but documented occurrence, the fetus had merged with Namyatov's while they were still in the womb and had never developed. Some of Namyatov's neighbors, newspapers reported, were disappointed that doctors had removed it. "They should have waited to see what would become of it later on," one said.

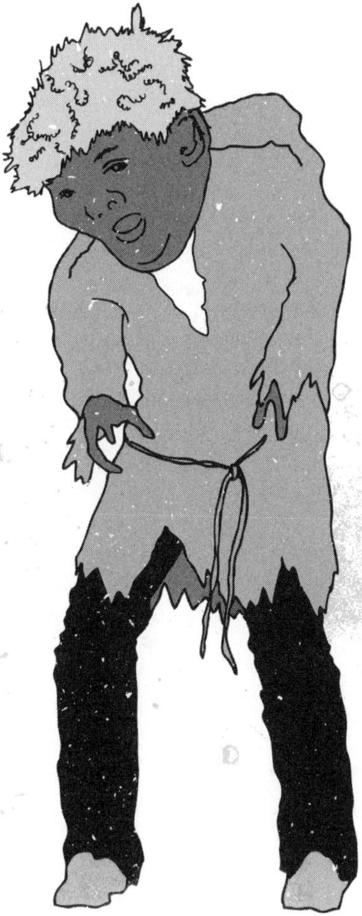

TYPHOID MARY

Whether you're the first man to set foot on the moon, to cross the finish line in the 100-meter dash at the Olympics, or to make a comment on an Internet article, it's great to be first. Yes, it's a thrill to be able to call out "First!"–except maybe if you're the first asymptomatic carrier of the pathogen associated with typhoid fever.

Mary Mallon was an Irish immigrant who worked as a cook in New York City in the early twentieth century. It's believed that she contracted the disease in one of the many family homes she worked in. But she was an asymptomatic carrier, meaning that she showed no signs of the deadly disease while unknowingly spreading it to others. The New York City Health Department eventually tracked her down and locked her away in an involuntary quarantine.

Typhoid Mary, as she was called by the media, would admit to the police that she rarely washed her hands before cooking food. Mallon was eventually released under orders that she not work as a cook, but she soon returned to her old occupation, because that was the only thing she knew how to do. However, that job was at the Sloane Hospital for Women. After a serious outbreak there in 1915, health officials once again quarantined Mallon...where she stayed for the final 23 years of her life.

DANCE FEVER

The irresistible compulsion to dance was a favorite topic for most disco songs. But when real-life jitterbug fever struck the French city of Strasbourg, it was no boogie wonderland.

It began in July 1518, with a single woman dancing in the street, unable to stop herself. Her compulsion was evidently contagious—within a month more than 400 townspeople were afflicted. Speculating that this was some sort of infectious madness or demonic possession, city leaders were determined to help the victims get the dancing out their systems, a groovy variation on bloodletting or "walking it off." To this end, they built a wooden stage and hired musicians to provide suitable music night and day. As the phenomenon persisted, a number of victims died of heart attack, dehydration, or sheer exhaustion. Then, after a month or so, the afflicted began to recover, and the dancing petered away to nothing.

Modern historians have scoured contemporary records looking for the plague's cause. Mass hysteria has been suggested, as have other theories ranging from religious mania to ergot poisoning (which was a likely culprit of accusations of witchcraft in sixteenth century New England), but no single explanation has been entirely satisfactory. The cause of the phenomenon is still shrouded in mystery.

DANGEROUS DANCES

Imagine the panic, grief, and guilt of a parent whose child has developed a life-threatening tumor even before emerging from the toddler stage. Then imagine the horror of watching that child begin to twitch violently, roll his or her eyes uncontrollably, and lose the ability to speak. Such is the fate–if usually only temporary–of a child stricken with Kinsbourne syndrome, also known as *opsoclonus myoclonus*, or "dancing eyes–dancing feet syndrome."

Exceedingly rare, this autoimmune disorder occurs when antibodies released to fight a neuroblastoma (a cancerous tumor in the nervous system) or a virus end up attacking the brain as well. The condition is most frequently found in children with an average age of 19 months, though it has been seen in adult cancer patients as well. The disorder has accompanied tumors about half the time it has been diagnosed; in other cases, doctors suspect that the antibodies melted tumors before turning on the patients' brains.

Kinsbourne syndrome can result in a decreased attention span and loss of balance, lethargy, and drooling. Fortunately, the condition isn't fatal in itself, and many children who develop it find relief when their tumors are removed. However, a long delay before diagnosis can result in permanent brain damage.

DANGEROUS DOSES

Actor Dennis Quaid never imagined that he'd be reading medical journals, he told a National Press Club gathering in 2010, much less writing for them. But that's where he found himself, penning an article in the *Journal of Patient Safety* after a terrifying 2007 incident in which his newborn twins, Thomas and Zoe, received potentially lethal overdoses of a blood thinner at L.A.'s Cedars-Sinai Medical Center.

The twins, who had been readmitted to the hospital shortly after birth when they developed an infection, were given heparin, which wards off clotting. But the packaging for the infant-appropriate dose–10 units–and the adult dose–the substantially larger 10,000 units–was practically identical. A hospital worker inadvertently grabbed a package of adult heparin, and that's what the babies received. Their blood reportedly became water-thin, resulting in both external and internal bleeding, including, at one point, a six-foot spurt of blood from Thomas's umbilical-cord stump.

The twins were relatively fortunate; their blood finally resumed clotting normally after 41 hours. Quaid soon learned that three infants in Indianapolis had died in 2006 due to similar mistakes with heparin. He has established a foundation and made a film to advocate safer hospital practices. Cedars-Sinai has spent millions to upgrade its own safety procedures.

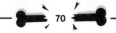

YOUR DOCTOR'S OFFICE IS BUGGED

As in it's crawling with germs, bacteria, and other microscopic nasties. Here are some sickening statistics about the cleanliness of clinics and hospitals that may convince you to think twice about picking up that ancient copy of *National Geographic* in the waiting room.

• **Over 1.7 million Americans** are admitted to hospitals every year. Around 100,000 of them die as a result of infections acquired during their stay.

• **The most common bacterial infection** picked up by patients is called *Clostridium difficile*. It causes flu-like symptoms, especially diarrhea, and accounts for around 20 percent of all hospital-acquired infections.

• **The average human hand** is covered in, literally, millions of germs. Oh, and an estimated 150 different species of bacteria are sitting on yours while you read these words. The vast majority of the bugs are harmless, but think about that the next time somebody's coughing near you in a waiting room.

• **It's impossible to determine** the average number of germs and bacteria that can be found on all the stuff in a typical doctor's office, but it could be well into the tens of millions. The dirtiest surface of all? Researchers say it's—unsurprisingly—the floor.

• **According to the Centers for Disease Control**, many strains of influenza can survive on surfaces for up to eight hours.

• **In 2012, England's National Health Service** advised clinics and hospitals to toss out their magazines after a week to help prevent the spread of diseases.

• **In 2011, researchers at the University of Maryland's School of Medicine** discovered that nearly half of the fifty hospitals they tested were littered with a strain of drug-resistant bacterium called *Acinetobacter baumannii*. They found strains of this nasty bug, which can cause infections and survive on surfaces for days, on everything from bed rails to tables and doorknobs.

• **"Neil," a $125,000 robot** created by Xenex Healthcare Services that underwent field tests at a hospital in Denver in 2013, could save medical facilities untold millions of dollars. It uses flashing ultraviolet lights to kill bacteria and germs.

• **The best ways to avoid getting sick** after a trip to your doctor's office? Bring your own magazine to read while you're waiting, avoid doorknobs, and—this should go without saying—wash your hands afterward.

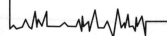

BLAME THE TOOLS

Seattle man Donald Church expected to be in pain following a 2001 surgery to remove a cancerous tumor, his appendix, and some intestinal material. But the pain seemed worse than he had expected. It hurt to move, it hurt to sit, and it hurt going to the bathroom, or it least it did the once a week or so when he could do that. Church told his doctors something was wrong, but they insisted he was enduring normal postsurgical pain.

Two months after the surgery, Church's wife found him collapsed on the bathroom floor. She took him to see Dr. Robert Morgan, who felt something odd in Church's abdomen. An X-ray revealed a metal surgical tool, roughly the size and shape of a ruler, had been left inside Church's abdomen.

The 13-inch retractor, which holds tissue and organs in place near an incision, is not usually fully inside the body, so it's rare that one would be left inside a patient. This one extended from the lower end of Church's pelvis up under his ribs and over his liver. It's remarkable that the retractor hadn't yet cut into Church's bowels or arteries, which would have caused a fatal bleed-out.

Church received a $100,000 settlement from the University of Washington Medical Center for the error…and had the retractor removed at a different hospital.

DUH VINCI

Having a prostatectomy—the complete and total surgical removal of the prostate—is the stuff of nightmares. But how about having one performed by an enormous four-armed robot? Or, worse yet, by a robot that's part of an "urgent medical device recall"?

The da Vinci Surgical System is a $2 million remote-controlled robot designed to perform minimally invasive surgeries, most commonly hysterectomies and prostate removals. Controlled by a human surgeon from a computer console, this drone doctor is equipped with tiny scalpels and electrocautery instruments (that's the process of zapping flesh with electricity to seal wounds, basically Terminator stuff).

Proponents argue that the robot is safer and causes fewer long-term side effects, like scarring. Unless, of course, it malfunctions as it did in 2013, when the da Vinci system more than doubled its total injuries and deaths. The robot had to be recalled from more than 1,300 hospitals.

The cause was simple—or as simple as anything is with a multimillion-dollar surgical robot. Friction in the robot arms caused the system to occasionally stall, interrupting its smooth surgical motion. And halting, jerky scalpels are a prescription for disaster when you're, say, having your uterus removed. The makers of da Vinci claim that there were only three instances of imprecise cutting out of 55,000 operations.

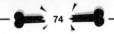

SECRET DOCTOR JARGON

Paging Doctor Blue. If you hear this over the public-address system, it means that doctors are stumped by a patient's problems and need more eyes in the hope that somebody will know something.

A.A.L.F.D. A patient faking symptoms in order to get painkillers, the acronym stands for "another a****** looking for drugs."

Betty. A diabetic.

Noctor. A nurse who acts as if he or she is more knowledgeable than the doctors.

D.B.I. score. Short for "dirt bag index," it's a number derived by multiplying the number of teeth a patient is missing by the number of tattoos, divided by how many estimated days it's been since the patient showered. The higher the number, the bigger the dirt bag.

C.H.A.O.S. "Chronic hurts-all-over syndrome," or a way doctors can let each other know that a patient has vague, undiagnosed pain or fibromyalgia.

A.L.S. While it might mean *amyotrophic lateral sclerosis*, or Lou Gehrig's disease, the doctor probably means a patient has an "absolute loss of sanity." In other words, he or she is nuts.

M.G.M. syndrome. A patient who is faking illness but really "putting on a show."

F.T.F. "Failed to fly"–an unsuccessful suicide attempt.

C.F.T. It stands for "chronic food toxicity," which is a gentler way of relating that a patient is obese.

Brothel sprouts. Genital warts.

Hi 5. The patient is HIV positive–V is the roman numeral for 5.

B.B.C.S. Bumps, bruises, cuts, and scrapes. In other words, the patient has no serious injuries.

A.T.D. A patient with this has overreacted about having a cold and thus has "acute Tylenol deficiency."

F.M.P.S. That's short for "fluff my pillow syndrome," referring to a hospital patient who isn't that sick but really likes the attention and sympathy.

Eiffel syndrome. When patients go to the emergency room to have something removed from their rectums (see page 84), they are too embarrassed to admit the real reason why something was in there, so the common response is "I fell on it." "Eiffel" = "I fell."

L.W.S. A patient with "low wallet syndrome" has no medical insurance or is too poor to pay.

Porcelain level. A doctor will ask another doctor to order this imaginary blood test to let them know that the patient is, like a porcelain toilet, "full of s***."

SWITCHEROO

Hospitals take plenty of precautions to ensure that newborns aren't given to the incorrect parents, including taking baby footprints and issuing matching ID numbers for moms and babies. But every so often, babies are mixed up and given to the wrong parents.

Callie Johnson and Rebecca Chittum were switched after being born in a Virginia hospital—a fact discovered when both girls were three years old. Tragically, Callie's biological parents, Kevin Chittum and Whitney Rogers, were killed in a car wreck before they could learn the truth; despite lawsuits, both girls remained with the mistaken (but loving) families.

Incredibly, there are also several documented cases of *twins* being separated at birth. In 2001 girls born in the Canary Islands each discovered a long-lost sibling while out shopping. A friend of one was working in a clothing store when one day the other twin came in. The friend tried to greet her with a kiss—but the girl refused, because she was the wrong twin.

And in Canada, George and Marcus Cain only discovered the accidental swap when both happened to attend Ottawa's Carleton College and were introduced by a mutual friend. When the two ended up meeting each other's families, it came to light that they had similar backgrounds; as it turns out, the two had been separated while in foster care.

BLOOD, RUSH

Benjamin Rush was one of the Founding Fathers and a signer of the Declaration of Independence. He believed all men had an inalienable right to life, liberty, the pursuit of happiness, and that most diseases could be cured by draining 80 percent of the blood from the body.

When an epidemic of yellow fever struck Philadelphia in 1793, Rush grew frustrated at the number of patients who were dying due to the conventional, outmoded treatment of fluids and bedrest. He discovered the research of a doctor from Virginia who speculated that bloodletting might be an effective treatment. Rush began with small bleedings, but soon his faith in the practice became something more like religious fervor. He would drain 20 ounces in a sitting, and sometimes nearly a gallon of blood over a week. His front lawn, where he dumped all that blood, reportedly reeked and the air was thick with flies.

Despite mounting evidence that bloodletting was not an effective treatment, and charges that he killed more patients than he saved, Rush remained devoted to the practice and even insisted on undergoing it himself shortly before his death. In 1904, the American Medical Association erected a statue of Dr. Rush in Washington, D.C., which still stands today. It makes no mention of bloodletting.

SCREWED

In 2001, spinal surgeon Robert Ricketson was performing a backbone operation on Arturo Iturralde, an elderly minister, at Hawaii's Hilo Medical Center. What happened next depends on whom you ask. According to Ricketson, his operating room was all out of the titanium rods he was supposed to insert into Iturralde's compromised backbone—apparently he skipped the presurgery inventory check. With Iturralde cut open on the table in front of him and with no other choice, Ricketson looked around the room, desperate for an alternative, and found a screwdriver. He removed the handle with a hacksaw (which, it should be noted, was more readily available than a titanium rod), then inserted the makeshift rod into Iturralde. Since it was roughly the appropriate size, the doctor figured it was a reasonable substitute.

"DESPERATE FOR AN ALTERNATIVE, HE FOUND A SCREWDRIVER.

A nurse and others in the O.R. tried to stop him, urging Ricketson to wait until a proper rod could be brought in from another of Hawaii's many hospitals. Ricketson reportedly ignored their qualms, insisting that it would be too dangerous to keep Iturralde under anesthetic for several more hours. After the operation, he allegedly told everyone in the O.R. not to tell Iturralde's family about the screwdriver.

Unsurprisingly, the shaft snapped in two a few days later. Ricketson then performed a second surgery and removed the pieces from his patient's back. Flabbergasted, his nurses retrieved them from a trash can and contacted an attorney on Iturralde's behalf. He didn't live long enough to witness his family's lawsuit against Ricketson–he died in 2003 after his health declined following a third unsuccessful surgery (by another surgeon) that left him a bedridden paraplegic.

Ricketson, forever with the do-it-yourself-spirit, defended himself at his malpractice hearing. He placed the blame on the attending surgical nurse, who, he claimed, assured him that they had all the surgical supplies necessary. Ricketson insisted that he had done what he had done to save his patient's life.

The jury was unconvinced, especially after learning that his medical license had been suspended in Oklahoma and revoked in Texas for, among other things, several malpractice suits and a nasty habit of writing himself prescriptions for painkillers. At the end of the five-week trial, the jury found the Hilo Medical Center 35 percent liable for the incident and Ricketson 65 percent liable. They awarded Iturralde's family $5.6 million in damages.

THE DOZING DENTIST

Nobody likes going to the dentist. They're close talkers you can't escape who torture your mouth while making chitchat. That's probably why most patients choose some form of general anesthesia for serious dental procedures—why not nap during a root canal? It's a great strategy for the patient, not so much for the dentist.

According to a suit filed in New York state court, a Brooklyn dentist named Isaak Grinman (a great dentist name notwithstanding) allegedly had the habit of sleeping through his procedures. For almost two years, Dr. Grinman slept while his unlicensed assistant—a college student—performed practically every filling and root canal at the practice. If college students can't even have candles in their dorms, they probably shouldn't be performing surgery. But for hundreds of patients, that's exactly what happened.

In fairness, there were often too many appointments in a day for Grinman to nap through them all. So he filled out his schedule by watching movies, running errands, and going on vacation. When he had to attend a continuing-education class required to keep his dental license, he sent an impostor to that, too.

The worst part of it all is that many of the procedures he skipped were unnecessary—he gouged his patients' wallets while his assistant gouged their impacted molars.

A CAPPY ACCIDENT

You've just got to wonder about dentists. What kind of person enters into a line of work that involves scraping the insides of other people's mouths, yanking out their teeth, and doing other things that make the profession generally feared and loathed? It's either the money (it's probably the money) or they really like pulling teeth. Sometimes, you've got to watch them.

In January 2013, Alecia White of Phoenix, Arizona, took her daughter, Savannah, to a local dentist to have four cavities filled. The girl was sedated and the cavities were filled. Then, after sending Alecia to the waiting room, the dentist kept going. Without asking Alecia, or even telling her, he placed shiny silver caps (crowns) on every tooth in Savannah's mouth.

Since the girl had been sedated, Alecia didn't notice what had happened until Savannah woke up at home, hours later. Both mother and daughter freaked out about the mouthful of metal. But the story does have a happy ending–after the Whites appeared on a consumer-activism segment on a local news show, another dentist offered to put realistic white veneers over the crowns to make Savannah look normal again.

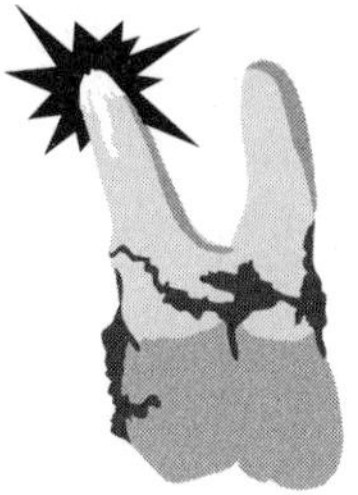

Of course, all of this was fairly unnecessary–the patient was four, and all of the teeth were baby teeth.

SMUGGLERS' BLUES

There are two kinds of people who smuggle drugs. "Drug mules" traverse the world with contraband hidden in everything from tires to lipstick containers. And then there are "body packers," who conceal narcotics inside their bodies by swallowing latex condoms or the fingers of rubber gloves that have been filled and sealed. If everything goes as planned, packers arrive at their predesignated drop-off point, where they stay until they "drop" their shipment into a toilet.

It's not a foolproof system. If the latex ruptures, the packer's system is flooded with potentially lethal doses of drugs. Or they just get caught.

• In 1982, a Colombian packer named Rosa Elvira Montoya de Hernandez was arrested at Los Angeles International Airport, and authorities found 88 containers of cocaine hidden in her gastrointestinal tract.

• Packers have become so prolific in Buenos Aires that a hospital near the city's major airport treats at least one packer with ruptured rubber every week.

• In 2002, a Ghanaian packer made it into the U.S. with 44 heroin-filled condoms in his stomach. Some ruptured, and he sought hospitalization. He sued the hospital for $25 million for permanently damaging his stomach. Case dismissed.

WE FOUND THIS IN YOUR STOMACH

A 10-pound hairball. In 2007, an 18-year-old woman had a mass of hair—which measured 15 inches by 7 inches—lodged in her stomach. The woman suffered from *trichophagia*—she eats her hair.

• **Magnets and steel.** Eight-year-old Haley Lents of Huntingburg, Indiana, nearly died after she ate steel marbles and magnets from a toy building kit...the attraction of which ripped eight holes in her intestines.

• **A key.** Eighteen-year-old Chris Foster had a bit too much to drink but didn't want the party to end, so he swallowed his house key—that way, he apparently reasoned, he wouldn't have to go home. He didn't remember any of that the next morning when he felt unusually sick. A quick X-ray confirmed the presence of the key in his stomach.

• **A diamond ring.** Simon Hooper didn't have the cash to pay for an engagement ring for his girlfriend, so he did the next best thing: He stole one and swallowed it. The plan backfired when police X-rayed his stomach, saw something suspicious, and kept him in jail until the £1,750 ring worked its way out.

• **An old pen.** Sometime in the mid-1970s, a British woman tripped and inadvertently swallowed a pen while examining her tonsils. A quarter-century later, doctors found the pen still embedded in the her stomach. The pen still worked.

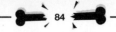

WE FOUND THIS IN YOUR RECTUM

For decades, urban legend has been flush with tales of items inserted into, stuck inside of, and/or rescued from the human rectal cavity, i.e., the butt. The most notorious items are small rodents of the hamster or gerbil variety and that wristwatch from *Pulp Fiction*. But along with the Internet's ever-expanding information glut has come a broader and bawdier assortment of verified stories about adventurers all too willing to test their intestinal fortitude.

• Living (and once-living) creatures remain popular, for some reason, from goldfish to a frozen pig's tail. One middle-aged man arrived at the emergency room claiming he had been trying to relieve constipation, which accounted for the live eel in his anus. Unfortunately, the eel went in headfirst, and the attendant chomping resulted in a perforated bowel that required surgery. Time with a colostomy bag: two months.

• That was easy time compared to the young fellow who inserted a half-full bottle of V8 into his colon… then made the mistake of going after it with a wire hanger, shredding his lower intestine. He shouldn't have had a V8, because for him, a colostomy bag is forever.

• Speaking of hard time, the penal system is replete with tales of new inmates who tried to make life a little cozier by smuggling objects into the hole via, um, the hole. One cavity search revealed the following inventory: a couple weeks' worth of oxycodone; a cigarette, matches, and a flint; an empty syringe (with an eraser covering the needle, thank goodness); ChapStick; a condom...and, of course, the receipt for these purchases, along with a coupon for his next visit to the store.

• A British veteran of WWII, suffering from hemorrhoids, found he could relieve his pain by using an artillery shell to shove the offending growths into his rectum. One day, however, he used too much force. And when he had to admit to ER doctors that the shell was live, a bomb squad was brought in to help remove it.

• Then there was the attorney who couldn't spend five minutes without his cell phone at his side–even in the shower. One unfortunate slip, however, and the phone was no longer beside him–it was inside him. The search-and-removal effort at the hospital was aided by the phone's frequent ringing.

+ + +

A HARD PILL TO SWALLOW

A doctor can earn upwards of $160,000 a year... in bonuses from drug companies if he prescribes the company's drugs enough.

RUMORS OF MY DEMISE...

In the New Testament, Jesus brings his friend Lazarus back to life after Lazarus has died and been laid to rest in his tomb. Likewise, in several documented cases, people who have been pronounced clinically dead with no pulse have come back to life in the hospital bed, or even hours later in a morgue or funeral home. This is rightfully known as the "Lazarus phenomenon."

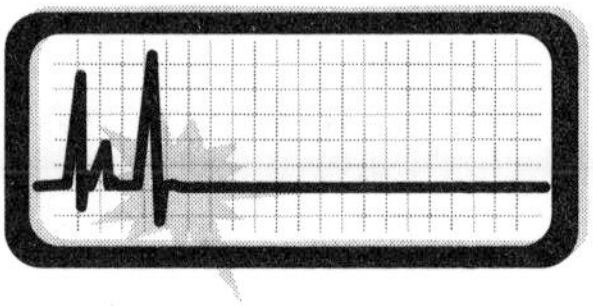

In 2007, a woman from Delaware was pronounced dead almost 90 minutes before she was noticed to be breathing in the morgue. A woman in Columbia was thought dead for more than two hours. When a funeral-home worker made an incision to insert formaldehyde, the "dead" woman began moving her arms. In the last 30 years, at least 38 cases of the phenomenon have been reported. The exact cause is unknown, in part because the phenomenon itself is so rare. Some suspect it could be the result of pressure released from the chest cavity following resuscitation or a side effect of high doses of epinephrine.

In the Bible, the resurrection of Lazarus is hailed as a miracle and a sign of Christ's divinity. In most documented cases of the Lazarus phenomenon, the experience leads to serious brain injury and other side effects—and often the filing of malpractice lawsuits.

NOT DEAD YET

Being an organ donor is one of the most generous things you can do. When you die, your organs are taken and given to people in desperate need of a kidney, liver, corneas, and more. Organ donation saves thousands of lives a year, "recycling" body parts that would otherwise go to waste. But it's important to make sure that the organ donors aren't still in need of those organs—for example, if they're still alive.

In 2009, a woman named Colleen Burns was rushed to the emergency room at St. Joseph's Hospital in Syracuse, New York, following an overdose of pills. Doctors examined Burns and determined that she had suffered heart failure. Burns's family was informed, and they authorized the hospital to remove Burns from life support and harvest her organs.

But Burns wasn't actually dead. An investigation later showed that doctors didn't perform enough of a brain scan on Burns, which is the kind of thing you do to check for brain death. Doctors also dismissed a nurse's reflex test of Burns in which her toes curled—another sign of life, as well as the fact that once Burns was taken off a respirator, she could breathe on her own. Doctors still decided to go ahead with the organ-harvesting surgery. It was called off only when Burns literally opened her eyes.

The hospital was fined $6,000 and told by the health department to hire a competent neurosurgeon.

DROPPED THE BALL

Benjamin Houghton entered a Los Angeles Veterans Administration hospital in April 2007 for a serious but all too common procedure: He was having a testicle removed because it was potentially cancerous. He left the hospital a few days later only to discover he'd been a victim of the ultimate switcheroo. Instead of the cancerous left testicle, the doctors had removed the healthy right (or rather, wrong) testicle.

Houghton was an Air Force veteran and father of four who had certainly seen some action in every sense of the phrase. However, he was ill-prepared for this nutty mix-up, which decreased testosterone production in his body and threatened depression, weight gain, and sexual dysfunction. As if the shame of losing a testicle isn't enough to create performance anxiety in the bedroom.

The hospital's chief of staff did offer an apology, but somehow we're thinking that wasn't quite enough. Houghton and his wife immediately filed a claim with the VA hospital for $200,000 to recoup medical costs and an "undisclosed amount" in pain and suffering.

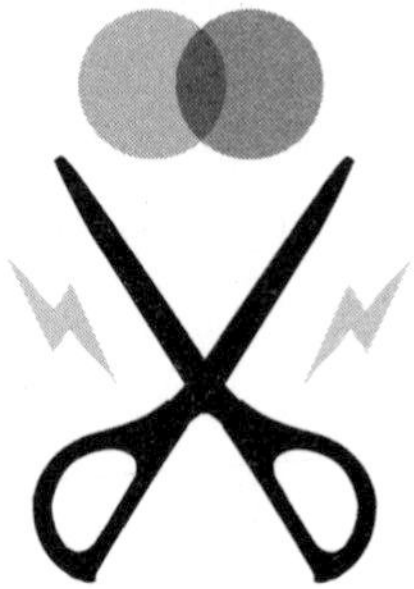

Houghton still had to have the cancerous testicle removed.

BIGGER, BUT NOT BETTER

The moral of this story: You will *never* find a quality medical professional advertising in a bar. Certainly not in New Jersey.

That's where 22-year-old Justin Street learned about the services of Kasia Rivera, who provided "beauty services" (primarily silicone injections) from the comfort of her home. Street wasn't happy with his, uh, personal endowment and after learning of Rivera's service via an ad at a neighborhood bar, asked Rivera for some enhancement.

Within a day, Street was dead. Turns out that because the penis is so packed with veins, it's a dangerous place to inject anything, let alone silicone. The silicone was absorbed into his bloodstream, spread throughout his body, and shut down his organs.

Not surprisingly, Rivera had no medical training, nor was she even a cosmetologist licensed to dispense silicone injections.

Okay, maybe one more moral to this story: There's no such thing as a foolproof penis enhancement. "If there were a legitimate method for penile lengthening, Johnson & Johnson or Pfizer would have bought it up and made billions and billions of dollars worldwide," said Dr. Daniel S. Elliott, an associate professor of urology at the Mayo Clinic. "The fact that they don't means it does not exist."

APPENDECTO-ME

If you were in excruciating pain that could lead to your death, would you have the wherewithal to man up, cut into your own body, and remove your own appendix? Leonid Rogozov did.

As part of a Soviet expedition to Antarctica in April 1961, Rogozov was working as a doctor at the Novolazarevskaya polar base alongside 12 other men. Since it was Antarctica, the base was remote and the weather tremendously awful. The conditions were such that airplanes couldn't fly in, and the terrain was too difficult to traverse by automobiles.

Rogozov had limited medical equipment and was the only man on base with any medical training, which must have made it pretty scary when he started running a high temperature and experienced nausea, vomiting, and searing stomach pain. He diagnosed his ailment as acute appendicitis. "This is it. I have to think through the only possible way out: to operate on myself. It's almost impossible, but I can't just fold up my arms and give up," he wrote in his diary. After two days of pain, Rogozov decided to perform the surgery on himself.

He enlisted two co-workers to assist: a meteorologist and a mechanical engineer. Their duties consisted of handing instruments to Rogozov and holding a small mirror over his abdomen so that he could see where, on himself, he was cutting and digging.

The operation lasted one hour and forty-five minutes. Despite his weakened state, high fever, and extreme vertigo, Rogozov soldiered on, although he had to stop every five or six minutes to vomit and collect himself. Against all odds, Dr. Rogozov was successful. A journal entry made hours after the surgery read: "At the worst moment of removing the appendix I flagged. My heart seized up and noticeably slowed. And all that was left was removing the appendix."

Amazingly, Rogozov recovered in two weeks and continued to work at the base for one full year. When he returned home, Rogozov received the Red Banner of Labor award from the Soviet government and began his career as a professor of general surgery in St. Petersburg.

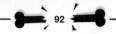

ACCORDING TO WebMD

We ran some mild, everyday health complaints through WebMD's "Symptom Checker." Here's what you probably don't have if you report one of these symptoms…but you might.

• Itchy? It could be body lice.

• Unexplained weight loss? It might be cystic fibrosis.

• Feeling stiff? It's possibly lupus.

• Feeling restless? It might be Lou Gehrig's disease.

• Got a bruise? That might mean massive internal bleeding.

• Mild joint aches could be a sign of Lyme disease.

• A rash may also indicate Lyme disease.

• Being overweight may be due to Cushing's syndrome, in which the body is unable to properly regulate or be exposed to cortisol.

• Feeling hot and sweaty at night might be tuberculosis or kidney cancer.

• Thirsty? You may have an overactive pituitary gland.

• Dry skin on your arms might mean you have an overactive thyroid gland.

• Flushed skin? It could be cyanide poisoning or West Nile virus.

• A bald spot may be the result of trichotillomania, a psychological disorder that makes you want to pull out your own hair.

• Pale skin may mean you have anemia or a vitamin B_{12} deficiency.

• Got a feeling of general weakness, or you're tired? It might be congestive heart failure or gastrointestinal bleeding.

+ + +

A MIST OPPORTUNITY

In 2008, a 39-year-old man checked into a hospital in the Philippines to have a "canister of perfume" removed from his colon (no word on how or why it got there). A team of doctors and nurses removed the canister...and filmed the procedure...and then uploaded it to the Internet. The film, which featured doctors and nurses laughing around the patient's unconscious body and cheering when they finally extracted the canister, became a viral hit. A hospital spokesperson later said that cameras and cell phones had been banned from operating rooms, and that it had been "a violation of ethical standards" for them to spray the perfume at the end of the video.

THE WORST HOSPITAL IN ENGLAND

In 2007 Bella Bailey, 86, of Staffordshire, England, checked into Stafford Hospital, the local facility. Almost immediately, she and her daughter, Julie, were terrified. Elderly patients moaned and screamed in agony. Hours would go by without any doctors or nurses stopping in to check on them, bring water or medication, or change bed linens. Julie Bailey's complaints to hospital authorities were ignored.

After eight weeks of inattentive care at Stafford, Bella Bailey died. So Julie Bailey created Cure the NHS, a group devoted to bringing attention to what she suspected were widespread, systemic failures at Stafford Hospital as well as at the NHS branch that oversaw it, the Mid Staffordshire NHS Foundation Trust. After her account was published in local newspapers, she received dozens of calls and letters from others who had witnessed similar lackluster treatment at Stafford.

It was worse than Bailey could have imagined. Stafford Hospital became the center of the biggest medical scandal in English history. Over the next few years, crown attorney Robert Francis, along with the Care Quality Commission and the UK's Department of Health, conducted a number of investigations into Stafford Hospital.

In 2010 Francis published a report stating that the hospital "routinely neglected" patients due to extreme cost-cutting measures instigated by the Mid

Staffordshire Trust. Later that year, the CQC found that Stafford fell short on 11 legally binding key standards of hospital safety and quality. It issued a warning to the trust: Low staffing levels were compromising patient quality. The trust was ordered to improve the hospital…or else.

But the trust continued to operate Stafford as it pleased. Then, in December 2011, it announced that due to staff shortages, it would close its emergency-clinic department for three months. Timing was key–the latest 139-day investigation into Stafford Hospital had just ended. The results: 164 witnesses testified and 87 others gave written statements–"appalling conditions" doesn't quite do it justice.

• There were numerous accounts of patients left to sit in urine-soaked or feces-covered bedsheets for hours. One long-term patient reportedly wasn't washed for a month.

• Frequent dispensation of the wrong drugs was a problem. One nondiabetic patient was given insulin, for example, and a patient allergic to opiates was given an opiate-based medication.

• Patients had food trays left out of their reach, and there were patients so thirsty they had to drink water out of flower vases.

• Buzzers to nurses were ignored, either by nurses who didn't care, nurses too busy to respond, or because there wasn't anyone at the nurses' station to respond.

• Decisions about treatment order or who to treat were left to receptionists, who were instructed to act on a "gut feeling" about severity of sickness or injury.

• Nurses wouldn't use or would switch off medical equipment they didn't know how to use, including heart monitors.

• Since senior doctors cost more to hire, Stafford's doctors were primarily inexperienced junior doctors just out of medical school, with limited emergency or surgical experience. If they needed a consult, there were few veteran doctors to ask–so they'd go to the nurses.

Why did the hospital operate in such a careless, callous manner? Money. More than 160 jobs at Stafford Hospital had been cut since 2005, when the trust's chief executive, Martin Yates, decided to secure for the hospital "foundation trust" status. That's a government policy that allowed the most economically efficient hospitals to set some of their own rules, apart from the country's rigid government-set regulations for hospitals. Chief among those freedoms: foundation-trust hospitals could set their own executive pay levels.

In order to get foundation-trust status, Stafford had to meet key requirements to show–or at least make it seem like–it was a well-oiled machine. One of those targets was a four-hour turnaround for emergency patients from the time they walked in to the time of treatment, full admittance, or discharge. The trust instructed hospital staff, with the threat of termination, to meet that limit by any means necessary.

• Doctors ignored critically ill long-stay patients to treat patients with minor emergencies, so as to get them out in four hours.

• Nurses were told by senior staff to falsify wait times in hospital records to make treatment times fall under the four-hour limit.

• Patients still waiting (but on the brink of the four-hour limit) were routinely placed in the "clinical decision unit," a loophole in the wait-time target. No real care was given, but it allowed nurses to file the patients as treated in less than four hours.

In addition to the inquiries, two incidents at Stafford Hospital became the basis of criminal investigations. In one, a four-month-old baby was found with a pacifier taped to his mouth. The other incident involved a 66-year-old woman who checked into the hospital in 2007 for treatment of a broken arm and pelvis. She wound up slipping into a coma and dying—she was diabetic, and nobody administered her insulin for 10 days.

In late 2013, the National Health Service decided enough was enough. It dismantled the Mid Staffordshire Trust and put management of the hospital into the more capable hands of University Hospital of North Staffordshire. But the damage was already—and thoroughly—done. According to the investigations, between April 2005 and March 2008, there were as many as 1,200 people who unnecessarily died at Stafford Hospital.

YOU DON'T NEED HALF A BRAIN

Basic logic would dictate that removing half, or even part, of somebody's brain is not a good idea. But this process–which is known as a *hemispherectomy*–has been proven to eradicate seizures in tough cases while preserving or even improving a person's quality of life.

It sounds hard to believe, but doctors have decades of research and anecdotal evidence to back it up. Hemispherectomies on children work because their brains are at peak *neuroplasticity*–existing neurons can compensate for the lost ones and can learn how to do things once handled by the missing half. Even older patients benefit from the surgery because the brain is so adept at bouncing back from trauma.

There are two types of hemispherectomies. In the anatomic version, doctors remove an entire brain half. The functional kind involves the removal of a portion of the brain and the severing of the *corpus callosum*, the series of neurons that link the two halves of the gray matter. The biggest potential downside: a loss of vision or mobility impairments on one side of the body.

Otherwise, it seems to work just fine. Of the 111 children who underwent the surgery at Johns Hopkins between 1975 and 2001, all remained seizure-free, or reduced their need for seizure medication.

EXPLODING HEAD SYNDROME

It's not as bad as you think…but it's still pretty bad. Most folks routinely awaken peacefully even when their sleep has been filled with horrors—nightmares that seem deathly real as they unspool but are blissfully forgotten by morning. But for an unlucky few, sleep is occasionally accompanied by ear-splitting sounds that seem to emanate from—and remain contained within—the sleeper's own mind. This form of auditory hallucination has come to be known as exploding head syndrome, and while it seems quite harmless physically, its impacts are only beginning to be understood by doctors.

Exploding head syndrome is experienced as a cataclysmic noise, similar to a bomb exploding, a gun firing, a crash of cymbals, etc. It typically occurs during the first couple hours of sleep, but is not necessarily part of a dream. The noise may be accompanied by a perceived flash of light and by momentary anxiety or an increased heart rate. Researchers have been unable to pinpoint why or how these phenomena occur, though they have established that the syndrome is slightly more prevalent in women than in men, and in adults over age 50.

The most common side effect, as one might imagine, is insomnia.

THE BLUNDERFUL WORLD OF (DR.) OZ

Dr. Mehmet Oz is a Harvard-trained physician and a professor of surgery at Columbia University. He has authored hundreds of scholarly articles. After making weekly appearances answering medical and health questions on *The Oprah Winfrey Show*, Oz got his own daily talk show, *The Dr. Oz Show*, in 2009.

More than three million people watch *Dr. Oz* every day, and his advice and influence are powerful. For example, when he recommended neti pots for nasal irrigation, sales of neti pots rose by more than 12,000 percent. But take his advice with a grain of salt—he's a busy man and has to fill five hours of TV every week, so not everything he says is going to be golden or, more importantly, accurate.

• On an episode airing in April 2012, Dr. Oz introduced his "heated rice footsie" as a way to cure insomnia. How to do it, said Oz, was to take a pair of socks, fill them with uncooked rice, microwave them for a few minutes, and wear them to bed. Frank Dietl, 76, had trouble sleeping, so he took Oz's advice, and made some footsies. However, Dietl has type 2 diabetes and suffers from neuropathy—a pronounced decrease of feeling in his feet. Dietl indeed fell asleep with the footsies on, and then he woke up…with second- and third-degree burns on his feet. Dietl sued Dr. Oz, mentioning in his suit that *The Dr. Oz Show* should have had a disclaimer for people with neuropathy. The suit was ultimately dismissed, with a judge ruling that a TV doctor addressing his anonymous audience didn't constitute a doctor-patient relationship, and thus Oz wasn't responsible for Dietl's injuries.

• On a 2012 episode, Dr. Oz recommended oral capsules filled with powdered green coffee beans as a weight-loss aid. Oz cited a study claiming that participants lost an average of 17 pounds in 22 weeks. The trial he cited had used just 16 people, far less than the hundreds used in normal drug trials, so the trial was not very legitimate. Also rendering his endorsement suspect was the fact that the study was funded by Applied Food Sciences, Inc., a manufacturer of green coffee bean supplements.

• Also in 2012, Dr. Oz touted garcinia extract, an acid found in mangosteen, as a natural fat burner. This was not a brand-new concept, nor was it real. Several studies had been made on garcinia since 1998, all of them deciding ultimately the same thing: that it was no more effective than a placebo.

• Dr. Oz writes books, too. In his pregnancy guide, *YOU: Having a Baby*, Oz warns mothers to "opt out until more data are available" with regards to vaccinating newborns against the deadly rotavirus because of a chance that the shot could lead to a severe intestinal problem called intussusception. A link between the vaccine and intussusception has been widely dismissed by the American Academy of Pediatrics, the Centers for Disease Control, and the World Health Organization.

IT'S PRIMAL

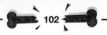

Bottling up your emotions isn't good for you; that's just common sense. But according to advocates of primal therapy, the effects can go far beyond headaches and grinding teeth. Repression, they claim, can cause a slew of physical and mental maladies.

Primal therapy was pioneered by Arthur Janov in the early 1970s. Janov taught that we are all marked by pain felt early in life—usually a lack of love in childhood—and that internalized pain manifests itself in a range of illnesses, including high blood pressure, cardiac arrhythmia, ulcers, phobias, depression, and autoimmune disorders like allergies and asthma. By regressing to an infantile state, the patient can confront and release this pain, exorcising it with a cathartic "primal scream."

The therapy has always been controversial. Its claims of a single universal root cause for a vast range of seemingly unrelated illnesses (and of the efficacy of a single treatment against all of them) strikes many diagnosticians as overly simplistic. But the method has some serious cultural clout, thanks to devotees like John Lennon, who wrote some of his most powerful solo material while undergoing treatment. "Shout," the 1984 hit by Tears for Fears, is about primal therapy.

So shout! Shout! Let it all out!

CLAIM DENIED

Peggy Robertson of Centennial, Colorado, was covered by her husband's health plan until he changed jobs in 2007. The family's new carrier, Golden Rule, deemed Robertson an "unacceptable risk" because her second child was born by cesarean section. According to Golden Rule, that increased the odds that she'd need to have a cesarean again, and they didn't want to have to pay for that. The only condition under which they would cover her at all was if she agreed to be sterilized. Robertson chose to opt out of health insurance.

• The Scaglione family of Lake of the Pines, California, applied for group family medical coverage in 2009. According to BlueShield's records, the mother, Valerie, suffered from a skin disease called rosacea. "I've never had that a day in my life," she said. BlueShield also claimed that one of her daughters, Samantha, once had bronchitis. That wasn't true, either. Valerie figured it was a "glitch in the system" and asked BlueShield to adjust their records. The company refused. The Scaglione family ended up paying more than $2,000 per month for coverage.

• One night in 2008, a 45-year-old woman was at a bar in Fort Lauderdale, Florida, when a man that she had met there gave her a "knockout drug." She awoke the next day fearing she may have been sexually assaulted. As a precaution, her doctor prescribed an anti-HIV drug. A few months later, the woman applied for health coverage with a new provider. Upon seeing her medical records, the insurer assumed she had a preexisting condition–HIV–and refused coverage. She was told she could reapply in four years, once it was clear that she was HIV-free. Today she wonders whether she should have taken the medication in the first place: "I'm going to be penalized my whole life because of this."

• Six-year-old Madison Leuchtmann of Franklin County, Missouri, was born without ear canals. In November 2009, the kindergartener was about to outgrow a headband device that gave her very rudimentary hearing. Madison's doctor said she needed permanent devices implanted inside her ears before she turned seven or she might never be able to hear again. Cost of the implants: $20,000. Cigna HealthCare refused to pay for the implants, claiming, "Hearing-assistance devices are not medically necessary."

• Rosalinda Miran-Ramirez woke up one night in 2009 to discover that her nightgown was covered with blood–she was bleeding from her left nipple. Her husband rushed her to the emergency room, where doctors discovered a tumor and performed a biopsy. Thankfully, the tumor was benign. BlueShield of California refused to pay the $2,791 emergency-room charges. The company insisted that Miran-Ramirez's decision to go to the emergency room was "not reasonable" because her bleeding breast did not constitute a “real emergency.” Miran-Ramirez contacted a local television station, KPIX-TV, in San Francisco and told her story on the news. “I am not a clinical person,” she said, “but if your breast is bleeding, for me that’s an emergency.” Amid all of the negative press, BlueShield “reassessed the claim” and covered the ER visit.

• In 2007 Nataline Sarkisyan was 17 years old and suffering from leukemia. She received a bone-marrow transplant from her brother, but there were complications, and her organs began to shut down. Doctors told her parents that she needed a liver transplant—soon—or she would die. Nataline was placed on a waiting list for a liver, pending her health insurer’s approval. Cigna refused to cover the cost of the transplant because it was “outside the scope of the plan’s coverage” and Nataline had “little chance of surviving the procedure.” Her doctors appealed, claiming she had a 65 percent chance. Cigna still refused. Nine days after the initial request, Nataline’s family—along with 120 members of the California Nurses Association—protested at Cigna’s Glendale offices. While the demonstrators shouted outside, Cigna agreed to make a “one-time exception” and cover the costly procedure. But it was too late—before the operation began, Nataline died.

THE EARLY AIDS CRISIS CRISIS

The mysterious and lethal virus that ultimately became known as HIV began terrifying the world in earnest in the early 1980s. But scientists believe it originated in Africa in the 1930s, in a species of chimpanzee indigenous to the continent.

Scientists eventually concluded that when hunters encountered blood tainted with the so-called simian immunodeficiency virus (SIV), they contracted the disease; it morphed into human immunodeficiency virus (HIV). This spread around the world over the coming decades but started becoming an epidemic in the U.S. in the early 1980s, when people—at first mainly gay and bisexual men and intravenous drug abusers—started developing what became known as acquired immunodeficiency syndrome, or AIDS.

Eventually, a link was established between HIV and AIDS, although doctors and other health professionals struggled to quell the spread of the virus for the rest of the decade. By 1989 just under 116,000 men and women in the U.S. had been diagnosed with AIDS; more than half had died.

That rapid spread coincided, or was helped along, with little to no acknowledgement by the government. It wasn't until September 1986 that government health officials mentioned AIDS in public—a full four years after the CDC mentioned the disease in its "Morbidity and Mortality Weekly Report."

Silence about AIDS wasn't the only damning action of the Reagan presidency. From a research standpoint, fighting the disease was severely underfunded–between June 1981 and May 1982, the CDC spent less than $1 million on AIDS...and $9 million on Legionnaire's disease, even though at that point the former killed 20 times more people than the latter.

Still, this imbalance lingered throughout the decade. In *Encyclopedia of AIDS,* Raymond Smith describes an atmosphere that was, at best, resistant to studying the disease: "In late 1982, Congress allocated $2.6 million to be targeted for the CDC's AIDS research, but the Reagan administration claimed that the CDC did not need the money and opposed any congressional supplemental appropriations designed to fund federal governmental AIDS policy efforts." Congress went around Reagan and increased AIDS funding anyway during the ensuing years.

Despite robust activity all around the country where AIDS education, research, and prevention were concerned, Reagan didn't take any significant action until 1987, starting with a public speech in May and the launch of the Presidential Commission on HIV. Still, even this gesture occurred eight months after C. Everett Koop published *The Surgeon General's Report on Acquired Immune Deficiency Syndrome*–a report he was commissioned to write in 1986, five years after AIDS shook America to its core.

THE DOPE ON DOPE

Devotees of nineteenth-century literature have doubtless run across the word "laudanum," but very few have encountered the real thing, because the ubiquitous Victorian cure-all–which was once, incredibly, available without a doctor's prescription–is now a tightly controlled substance. Laudanum is a tincture, a precise blend of nine parts alcohol to one part powdered opium.

Insane as it seems, opium derivatives were once seen as all-purpose wonder drugs. With the pharmaceutical industry in its infancy–even aspirin wasn't invented until 1899–options for pain relief were limited, and potent narcotics were prescribed for every discomfort. Got a cold or hacking cough? Morphine will fix that right up! Arthritis? Rheumatism? Got you covered! Cramping? Diarrhea? You guessed it–laudanum! Colicky baby? Spoon some tincture of opium into him! Plus, if you just wanted to get really, really high, laudanum was cheaper than gin.

By 1907, opium's addictive properties were better understood, and new laws mandated that all narcotics be properly labeled. Interestingly enough, it was the labeling that drove laudanum off the market. Though it was still widely available, sales dropped by 33 percent once labeling was instituted. Seems that most people prefer not to be dope fiends, if they can help it.

THE RATTLESNAKE KING

Have you ever heard of the term "snake oil salesman," which refers to any kind of huckster who peddles a useless concoction as a cure-all medicine? Clark Stanley is the original snake oil salesman. He created a stir at the 1893 World's Fair by killing a live reptile during a demonstration of his product, Snake Oil Liniment. He claimed that the liniment, made of fats and body oils of snakes, was a Hopi cure for toothaches, stomach problems, and just about anything.

He traveled across the U.S., billing himself as "the Rattlesnake King," attracting large crowds eager to buy the mysterious Snake Oil Liniment, which he sold for the low, low price of 50 cents a bottle. It caught on, and Stanley mass-marketed Snake Oil…for more than 20 years.

Federal authorities finally caught on in 1915, after the passage of the Pure Food and Drug Act. They seized a shipment of Stanley's oils and discovered that the product didn't contain the slightest bit of snake (not that snake derivatives are really an effective medicine anyway). Snake Oil Liniment consisted of 99 percent mineral oil, 1 percent beef fat, and trace amounts of red pepper and turpentine.

For false advertising, Stanley was fined the steep, steep fee…of $20.

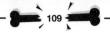

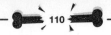

THAT HEALTHY RADIOACTIVE GLOW

Marie and Pierre Curie discovered radium in 1898, but it took decades of research for the long-term effects of radiation exposure to be understood. But in the interim, the general public regarded the stuff with almost superstitious awe. After all, it glowed with a beautiful phosphorescence! And if it was that miraculous, certainly it must be healthy.

Within a few years of its discovery, radium was—with no evidence whatsoever—being marketed as a restorative for youth and vitality. For that healthy glow, people used radium-laced toothpaste and face powder. Patients soaked in irradiated water to relieve rheumatism; heating pads loaded with radioactive ore soothed arthritis.

In particular, radium was reputed to cure sexual impotence. It shed its magical light in places where the sun don't shine as suppositories—and in the form of slender rods of radium-impregnated wax, to be inserted into the urethra. (Radium-dusted undergarments provided a less invasive option.)

So be grateful for those burdensome due-diligence regulations on the pharmaceutical industry. It may take years for innovative treatments to reach drugstore shelves, true—but that's the trade-off for making sure that your jockstrap doesn't give you cancer.

FULL OF IT

Let's say you suddenly came down with *C. difficile*, a bacterial infection that causes severe diarrhea and bowel inflammation. Your doctor said he had a miracle cure that proved effective 94 percent of the time. You're all for it, right? So, what if it involved inserting another person's feces into your body?

It turns out the "good" bacteria that exits your body through feces proves to be just the trick to help offset the "bad" bacteria that grows as a result of diseases like *C. difficile*. Hence the "fecal transplant," developed in part by Dr. Josbert Keller at the University of Amsterdam.

A "donor stool" is introduced into the GI tract, in most cases through colonoscopy, although enema and nasal tubes are alternative, *far* less appealing options. The good microorganisms that all of us require to keep our insides healthy start growing in the patient's colon and manage to crowd out and eliminate all the troublesome, unhealthy bacteria.

Although a fecal transplant sure sounds like perhaps the grossest procedure possible, it's hard to argue with the results—one study ended early because the transplants were so effective that it seemed unethical for doctors to withhold them from patients being treated with only antibiotics. Putting a little poop in sure seems to beat the alternative of lots of poop coming out. Maybe.

THE BULLET BABY

In 1863, a Southern family was watching the Battle of Raymond from the veranda of their house when their daughter, an unmarried virgin of great virtue, was struck in the side by a stray bullet. Dr. LeGrand Capers, a Confederate army doctor, examined her and determined that the wound was not life-threatening; he judged it best to leave the bullet fragment in place rather than attempt a risky abdominal surgery.

The girl made a full recovery…only to discover herself pregnant, and evidently miraculously so. Nine months after the Battle of Raymond, she gave birth to a baby boy. Stranger still, the smashed bullet was later removed from the infant's scrotum.

Dr. Capers recalled a soldier at Raymond who had been shot in the groin, the bullet carrying off one testicle. Neither bullet nor testicle had been recovered, and Capers theorized that the bullet—carrying on its surface a quantity of spermatozoa—had gone on to hit the girl's womb, producing her miracle baby. Capers introduced the soldier to the young mother; luckily, they hit it off and eventually married.

It's a famous piece of Civil War lore, but is it true? Not really. Dr. Capers, a prominent and respectable physician, wrote his account and submitted it anonymously to the *American Medical Weekly* as a satire of the fancifully exaggerated stories that the journal was regularly printing. The editor recognized Capers's handwriting, though, and—apparently wanting to show that he was in on the joke—printed the story with Capers's name attached, confident that readers would recognize it for the ludicrous fabrication that it was.

But some folks either have no sense of humor or believe everything they read—because the story was widely accepted as true, and slipped, unattributed, into history. Capers's article was cited in scholarly journals as late as 1959, and the gist of the story was still being circulated in popular reference books well into the 1970s.

Rumor, they say, travels like a speeding bullet while the truth is still getting its pants on. And it's been hard to lay this hoax to rest precisely because it is so over the top. It's not just too good to be true—it's so good that we want it to be true.

+ + +

TWO REAL FACTS ABOUT FAKE HEARTS

• The first artificial heart was implanted into a man in Texas in 1969. Made of synthetic Dacron fabric, it lasted three days.

• The first artificial heart valves were widely used in the 1950s. A tiny plastic ball would move, opening and closing off blood flow. That low-tech solution worked pretty well, except for one bizarre side effect: deafening clicks from the balls could be heard whenever a patient opened their mouth.

SYMPTOM FREE

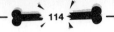

A*symptomatic* diseases are conditions without noticeable symptoms. So what's the problem with that? Symptoms are an alert; asymptomatic diseases wreak havoc until you finally do notice, at which point...it's probably too late.

HIV. Before it develops into AIDS, the HIV virus doesn't bring with it many symptoms at first, besides a possible brief and mild flu a couple of weeks after infection. After that, the patient feels fine and can then unknowingly spread the virus.

Celiac disease. The National Foundation for Celiac Awareness lists more than 300 symptoms of celiac disease, an autoimmune condition that damages the small intestine, rendering it unable to absorb many nutrients. Among them: bloating, gas pain, diarrhea, joint pain, headaches, fatigue, and discolored teeth. But it's asymptomatic in mild cases–the small intestine absorbs just enough nutrients so that symptoms don't occur. But people who don't know they have celiac disease still risk long-term health effects, including osteoporosis and thyroid problems.

Deep vein thrombosis. You can't feel a blood clot deep within a leg vein. Nor can you feel it when it travels through the bloodstream, lodges in your lungs, and causes a deadly pulmonary embolism. (That you can feel.)

Pancreatic cancer. This is widely considered to be one of the deadliest forms of cancer—because it's asymptomatic. Telltale symptoms, such as jaundice and sudden weight loss, only surface when the disease is in an advanced stage, at which point it's often too late to recover from.

Black urine disease. Clinically known as *alkaptonuria*, this condition is characterized by urine that turns brown or black if it's left out and exposed to air for a while. But who does *that*? Other than a slight darkening of the whites of the eyes, symptoms are sparse. Unchecked, alkaptonuria leads to a buildup of homogentisic acid in body tissue, which damages the cartilage around the spine and causes joint pain, lower back pain, kidney stones, and, in men, prostate stones.

Diabetic retinopathy. Premature blindness or vision loss is a well-known complication of diabetes, and it can come on suddenly for people who have had diabetes for decades. Otherwise, vision remains normal for years…until blurry vision kicks in one day and then gets progressively worse.

Balanitis xerotica obliterans. This infection takes time to make its presence known, manifesting as white patches and hardened tissue on the skin and foreskin (if the man is uncircumcised). That's when symptoms develop, which include irritation and problematic intercourse, at best, and urinary retention and bladder and kidney damage, at worst.

LET'S KILL PRESIDENT GARFIELD!

James Garfield was elected president in 1880, but it was a job he didn't really want. The nine-term Republican congressman was drafted by his party to run, so he felt obliged to serve.

This was the era of the "spoils system," before the Secret Service protection era, which meant that virtually anyone could go to the White House and request a job in the new presidential administration, whether they were capable or not. That's what Charles Guiteau did. He'd attempted several careers and failed at all of them, but still went to the White House several times, demanding to be appointed as an ambassador to France. Garfield personally turned him down. And that's when, Guiteau later said, God told him to kill the president.

On July 2, 1881, four months into his term, Garfield went to the Washington, D.C., train depot to travel to Massachusetts. Guiteau was waiting for him there, and shot the president almost immediately upon his arrival. He fired two shots: One missed the president's arm and the other lodged in his back.

Amazingly, the shot settled behind Garfield's pancreas but didn't puncture it, nor did it strike any vital organs or Garfield's spine. Today's modern medical technology, such as X-rays or scans, could immediately tell doctors this information. But this was 1881, when doctors had, comparatively speaking, no idea what they were doing.

Chaos ensued in the train station, and several doctors were called to the scene. The first made Garfield drink a cocktail of brandy and ammonia, which didn't help with the bullet wound at all and made Garfield vomit. Twelve doctors in all showed up to assess the president's condition, and all 12 took virtually the same approach: They stuck unsterilized and unwashed medical instruments, and their unsterilized and unwashed fingers, into the president's mangled back, just probing and digging around, in attempts to locate and remove the bullet. And all of this happened on the dirty floor of a train station.

At the time, American doctors had not yet adopted British doctor Joseph Lister's antiseptics protocols, which had been around since the 1860s. Nor did they believe that tiny things you can't see—germs—could cause disease, infection, and death. The prevailing thinking of the time was miasma theory: that bad air causes sickness. (This is why so many sick people in nineteenth-century novels were sent, almost always in an act of futility, to convalesce in the "fresh air" of the countryside.)

The second doctor on the scene immediately declared himself to be in charge of the whole operation: Dr. Doctor Willard Bliss. (Yes, his first name really was "Doctor.") Bliss was convinced, through shady eyewitness accounts, that the bullet had headed rightward into Garfield's back. He probed that channel with his fingers; he was wrong, but he did create a new tunnel in the president, which would soon fill with pus. Another handsy doctor accidentally punctured Garfield's liver.

Garfield was returned to the White House for recovery. His health rapidly weakened over the summer as, unbeknownst to the medical team, infection set it and spread. The infection weakened his heart. He had constant fevers, extreme pain, and hallucinations. His weight dropped from 200 pounds to 135. And throughout it all, Bliss and other doctors kept sticking their dirty fingers deep inside the president, looking for that pesky bullet that they thought was killing him, while introducing and putting in more germs that actually would kill the president.

Finally, Bliss summoned famed inventor Alexander Graham Bell to assist him. Bell had just invented something called the "induction balance," and Bliss thought Bell could use it to find that bullet. The induction balance was more or less a metal detector, but seeing as how Garfield lay on a metal bed, it didn't work very well. But because Bliss was still so convinced that the bullet had lodged on the right side of Garfield, he only allowed Bell to scan the right side of Garfield's body. The bullet was not found on the right side, because it wasn't there.

On September 6, 1881, Garfield was sent to a New Jersey beach house to recover (that "fresh air" was supposed to do him some good). Instead, sepsis and infection set in, as did angina. He died on September 19, 1881–80 days after he was shot.

An autopsy finally located the bullet. It was, Bliss's arbitrary conviction be damned, on the left side of Garfield's body. He also had pneumonia in both lungs, a body filled with pus, and infection-caused abscesses throughout. So Guiteau shot Garfield, "but his doctors killed him." That's a quote from Guiteau, shortly before he was hanged for his role in the president's death.

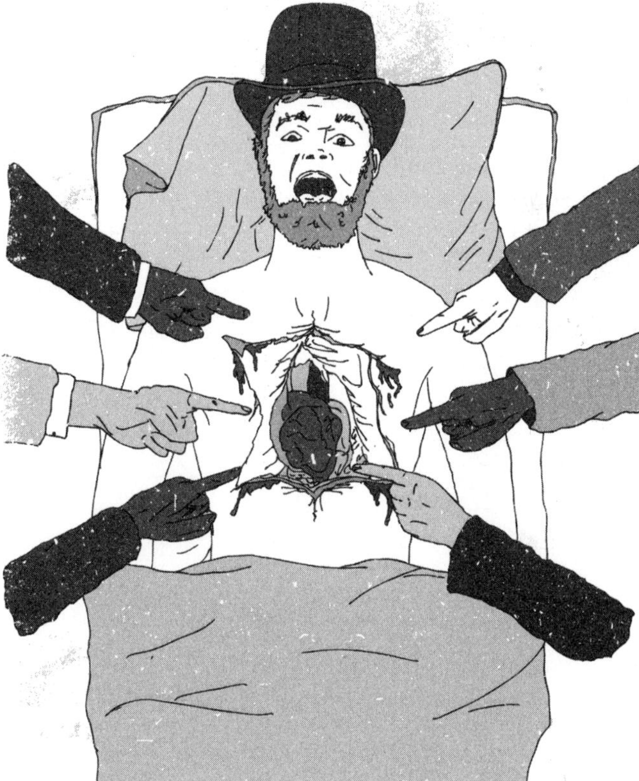

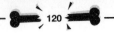

POOP FOR BRAINS

So far, you've read lots of stories in this book about doctors who have behaved in an unethical manner. But this one might be the worst incident of all…or at least the most disgusting.

In 2010 and 2011, two neurosurgeons working at the University of California–Davis Medical Center conducted a study to see if brain tumors could be killed by infections caused by fecal bacteria. The three individuals selected for the study were each suffering from end-stage *glioblastoma multiforme*, an aggressive brain tumor, and it would have taken a miracle or, at the very least, an aggressive experimental treatment, such as fecal bacteria, for them to survive.

So it's a little gross, and pretty far out there. They were prime candidates for the experiment, but the doctors made one big mistake: They didn't get the patients' permission. Actually, they made lots of big mistakes. According to documents from the California Health and Human Services Agency, both the surgeons and their support staff committed a series of additional blunders. They failed to adhere to various safety protocols, didn't bother following several regulations for pre- and postoperative surgical care, and hadn't adequately researched the fecal bacteria they were using. They also didn't get the required approval from the FDA. Particularly incriminating is that surgeons reportedly didn't label the containers of fecal bacteria as they were being stored or taken into the operating room, likely so as to not arouse suspicion.

The sickening story was discovered by journalists after the California State Department of Public Health's Center for Healthcare Quality announced a list of state hospitals facing penalties. Amazingly enough, this was the Davis Medical Center's first offense, which meant that it got off relatively easy. The facility was fined a meager $50,000 for their crappy experiment. The two surgeons resigned after an internal investigation determined that they "deliberately circumvented" federal regulations and internal policies set up to prevent things like doctors putting poop in people's brains.

+ + +

BI-OOPS-Y

Anica Kavecic, a seemingly healthy 50-year-old woman from Slovenia, complained to her doctor of severe stomach pains. Despite no history of gastric problems, Kavecic's biopsy suggested malignant cells had spread all over her stomach. She went under the knife soon thereafter, undergoing a complete gastrectomy—a stomach removal. Afterward, a lab thoroughly examined her stomach and found no evidence of disease, meaning that it had never been there in the first place. A pathologist had confused her biopsy results with those of a cancer patient.

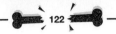

A HUMOUROUS STORY

Medieval doctors theorized that the human body is a sack filled with various fluids, which they called "humours." Perhaps observing how a test tube of blood will naturally separate into four layers, they identified four fundamental humours: black bile, blood, yellow bile, and phlegm. Of these four semi-imaginary substances, they decided, was the entire human body composed. It followed, therefore, that good health depended on these four humours being in proper balance. When the proportions of that mixture were out of whack—when one humour was dominant over the others—health suffered.

Each humour became associated with a particular organ (spleen, liver, gallbladder, or lungs, respectively), then with one of the four classical elements of earth, air, fire, and water—and by extension with the dualistic qualities of matter. Each element, and each humour, was defined as either cold or warm and either moist or dry. Blood, for instance, was identified with air, with warm and moist qualities, while black bile was associated with earth, cold and dry.

The system encompassed the entire physical world. Each humour was identified with one of the seasons, with a particular time of day, with certain plants, animals, and minerals. Every planet, every constellation, and every astrological sign had a corresponding humour. Even human psychology was explained by four basic personality types—melancholy, sanguine, choleric, and phlegmatic—all defined by a dominant humour.

It made for bad medicine. In theory, eating the proper foods would encourage production of a particular humour—but rather than topping off one humour, medieval physicians preferred to correct imbalances by draining any excess of the others. If there wasn't enough blood in your mix, for instance, enemas would be prescribed to reduce your black bile, along with induced vomiting to bring up yellow bile. A rubdown with blistering agents would release phlegm in the form of weeping pus. If too much blood was your problem, there was always bloodletting, sometimes accomplished by leeches. If treatments were ever effective, it was pretty much by accident.

Why did this system remain popular for hundreds of years, until it was finally displaced by the scientific method? Perhaps because it gave a framework of order to a chaotic universe and placed humankind at the center of it. This theory was very comforting to the medieval mind—even if it didn't actually work.

✚ ✚ ✚

A WORLD OF GERMS

In 2012, a team of biologists from North Carolina State University swabbed the belly buttons of 60 volunteers. They found 2,368 distinct species of bacteria. More than 1,400 of them had never been seen before.

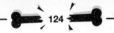

DIFFERENT STROKES

Happy and He Knows It

Malcolm Myatt suffered a stroke in 2004. He spent 19 weeks in the hospital recovering from the event, which struck the frontal lobe of his brain, in particular the area that regulates emotions. The ramifications: Ever since, he's been unable to feel sadness. He's constantly happy, even when attending funerals. Myatt's stroke also left him struggling with short-term memory loss, but he's reportedly too busy laughing to care too much.

Queer Circumstances

Englishman Chris Birch was a classic "punter," a rough-around-the-edges man's man, whose favorite activities were rugby and swilling pints at the pub. Then one day in 2011, in a freak accident, he took a tumble down a hill and had a stroke in the process. A year later, Birch's life had completely changed: He was a hairdresser, with dyed hair and a steady boyfriend. Birch did not identify as gay before the stroke, but today has little recollection, or interest, in his past life as a banker, nor in his female fiancée.

It All Comes Out in the Welsh

Alun Morgan learned a bit of Welsh when he lived in Wales for a few months during World War II. Yet the 81-year-old Englishman woke up from a stroke after a three-week coma and could speak only Welsh at first—and fluently. His command of English did come back gradually…and he managed to forget all of the Welsh he'd mysteriously "learned" (or unearthed) after his stroke.

Third Arm Blind

You may find yourself needing an extra hand from time to time, but nothing like what a 64-year-old stroke victim reported to her doctors—a pale, white, translucent "third arm," which she claims to be able to both see and control, even to scratch her cheek to relieve an itch. Known as a *supernumerary phantom limb*, the condition is typically reported in victims of arm or leg loss. The woman is the first known case of a person who can feel, see, and deliberately move a phantom limb.

Brain Food

An ultra-rare condition triggered only occasionally by strokes affecting the right-brain lobes, gourmand syndrome results in the patient becoming suddenly obsessed with fine dining and even specific fancy foods. One Swiss political journalist became a full-time food critic after suffering a stroke; in another case, a snowboarder suffered a severe head injury that left him with an inexplicable and constant craving for pesto.

PROBLEM VS. CURE

It's a very common TV commercial: Beautiful people frolic through the woods, holding hands, convincing us that a wonderful new pill can cure an annoying ailment. Then a pleasant-voiced woman quickly and quietly warns of all the rare but still possible—and horrible—side effects of that medication.

That warning is a legally sufficient consumer warning for most drugs. But not for isotretinolin, sold under the brand name Accutane. Roche, the manufacturer of this popular acne drug, is the only pharmaceutical company that requires patients to sign a consent form, agreeing not to sue over side effects, before they can get their prescription. The possible tradeoff for clear skin: complete hair loss, rectal bleeding, irritable bowel syndrome, and insanity.

The consent form is a direct result of a case involving former Accutane user Andrew McCarrell. Even though he took Accutane for only three months in 1995, he experienced tremendous stomach pain and bloody stools, which doctors diagnosed in 1996 as irritable bowel syndrome...a direct result of the Accutane (although he hadn't taken it in a year). It was so bad that McCarrell endured four surgeries to remove his colon and his rectum. Today, he wears a colostomy bag and still suffers from stomach cramps.

McCarrell sued Roche and was awarded $25 million. The presiding judge called it "the worst case of pain I have ever seen in my 18 years on the bench."

This is only one of the hundreds of lawsuits filed against Roche over Accutane by people who have developed conditions such as ulcerative colitis, bone loss, erectile dysfunction, hepatitis, heart failure, and blindness. And then there's the dementia. Since 1982, more than 1,370 psychotic episodes and 65 suicides among istotretinolin users have been reported to the FDA. Is beautiful baby-butt skin honestly worth the risk? Incredibly, every year 500,000 Americans say yes and sign away their rights to get their clear-skin pills.

+ + +

TWO REAL FACTS ABOUT FAKE HEARTS

Dr. Totada Shanthaveerappa, 70, of Atlanta, was arrested in 2005, accused of treating patients with unauthorized drugs and filing false insurance claims. The drugs: several not yet approved by the FDA, including dinitrophenol–a commercial weedkiller and insecticide–which Shanthaveerappa was injecting into patients. The strangest part, though, was that prosecutors couldn't claim that anybody was actually harmed by the treatments. Several people came forward and said that the doctor–who faces 87 counts in federal court–had actually saved their lives.

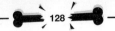

FROM MESMERISM TO HYPNOTISM

Hypnotism has had a hard road to medical acceptance. Although it can be a valuable therapeutic tool, it's also a parlor trick for making nightclub patrons cluck like chickens. And its origins are shrouded in superstition and quackery. Trances and visionary experiences have been known throughout recorded history; these quasi-hypnotic altered states of consciousness have been used in religious and healing rituals since the time of the pharaohs. But a scientific approach to hypnotism dates back only to the eighteenth century–and frankly, it wasn't particularly scientific even then.

An Austrian charlatan named Franz Mesmer became a sensation in 1778, founding a clinic in Paris where, he claimed, he could cure various ailments by manipulating the magnetic fields of the human body. Despite all Mesmer's tools, such as iron filings and tubs of "magnetized water," contemporary accounts indicate that his "animal magnetism" was, in fact, hypnosis.

Visitors to Mesmer's clinic reported bizarre behavior in patients under treatment. Mesmer gazed into their eyes and made "passes" with his hands; hysterical patients sobbed, convulsed, or had spasms of laughter, entirely oblivious to everything around them. (Prefiguring modern hypnotism's double life as therapeutic practice and performing art, Mesmer gave public demonstrations as well as private sessions, the former generally concluding with a musical number.) Mesmer was run out of Paris a few years later, but not before bequeathing to us the word *mesmerize*.

It was not until the 1840s that physicians began to explore the medical implications of mesmerizing. Scottish doctor James Braid gave hypnosis its name—from the Greek for "sleep"—and discovered posthypnotic suggestion, where commands implanted during the trance state carry over into consciousness. Braid also pioneered using hypnosis as an aid to breaking bad habits, like smoking.

Before the development of ether, hypnotism was also used for pain management. (And still is: Lamaze childbirth derives from hypnotic principles.) Civil War surgeons performed gruesome battlefield surgeries with only hypnotic suggestion for anesthesia. And Sigmund Freud famously used hypnosis in his treatments. But the discipline—still tainted by association with crooks like Mesmer—remained a fringe subject. It was not until the 1950s that the AMA formally embraced hypnosis as a full-fledged therapeutic technique.

✚ ✚ ✚

A NOT SO FUN FACT

Research shows that doctors misdiagnose patients as much as 15 percent of the time.

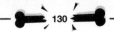

BACKGROUND CZECH

In 1983 Joseph Branda underwent surgery at Walson Army Hospital in Fort Dix, New Jersey. He needed a half-inch-long tumor removed from his bladder. It was supposed to be a fairly routine procedure, but in the middle of it, Branda stopped breathing. Surgeons didn't notice. A heart monitor would have alerted them to Branda's flatlining, except that the presiding anesthesiologist, Dr. Abraham Asante, had forgotten to hook one up.

After Branda had gone into cardiac arrest and his face and chest had turned blue, doctors noticed. They revived him, but to little avail–he had fallen into a coma from which he would never emerge. Branda died three years later.

An investigation by the U.S. Army into Asante's competence revealed that he was far from competent, namely because he wasn't really a doctor.

Asante emigrated to the United States from Czechoslovakia in the early 1970s and applied to the U.S. Educational Commission for Foreign Medical Graduates, which determines if foreign-born doctors may test to become doctors in the United States. That commission found Asante's Czech medical degree to be phony. But three states don't require certification by the agency to let foreign-born doctors take their licensing exams. So Asante tested in those three states–and he failed all of the tests. Multiple times, in fact.

But Asante practiced medicine anyway—with the U.S. Army. No one who ever hired him ever questioned his qualifications, or detected that his Czech medical degree was fake, or was aware that foreign-born doctors who wish to practice in the United States have to pass some tests and become certified. Asante, for his part, fooled doctors and patients alike by attending continuing-education courses for doctors looking to stay current with medical procedures.

After a number of medical jobs in the U.S. Army, Asante was promoted to anesthesiologist at Walson Army Hospital—as its only anesthesiologist. His ruse went undetected through hundreds of patients and successful surgeries, up until the debacle with Branda. In 1983 Asante was sentenced to 12 years in prison.

"Clearly, with hindsight, someone somewhere along the line could have and should have done a better job of guaranteeing that Mr. Asante was who he said he was. There will always be a lingering question as to who exactly should have borne that responsibility," a U.S. Army spokesman said.

✚ ✚ ✚

CRETE-TURE COMFORTS

Health officials on Crete ordered an investigation after the inspection of an operating room found a live scorpion. It came just a few weeks after a rat tail was found in a bowl of soup in another hospital.

LIKE DOOGIE HOWSER, BUT TERRIFYING

It would be shocking to learn that one of those doctors roaming the halls of a hospital was not fully trained and accredited, let alone a teenage dropout.

Frank Abagnale, who spun tales of his life as a teenage imposter into the book (and later movie) *Catch Me If You Can*, spent 11 months serving as chief resident pediatrician at a Georgia hospital. His job was primarily to supervise the interns—young doctors aspiring to be pediatricians (who were older than he was). When approached with a real medical question, Abagnale would defer to the interns, who took pride in the level of confidence Abagnale put in them.

Of course, Abagnale had no medical knowledge whatsoever and was also terrified by the sight of blood. He routinely made minor blunders, like walking into a nursery without washing his hands or putting on a mask. He claims it wasn't until the end of his tenure that he realized the risks of his deception. A nurse ran to him warning they had a "blue baby." Abagnale thought it was a joke and told her he had a green baby to deal with. It wasn't until he consulted his medical dictionary that he learned the term meant a baby whose blood lacked oxygen. By the time he got to the room, one of his interns had already arrived, bailing him out again.

LIKE DOOGIE HOWSER, BUT INCOMPETENT

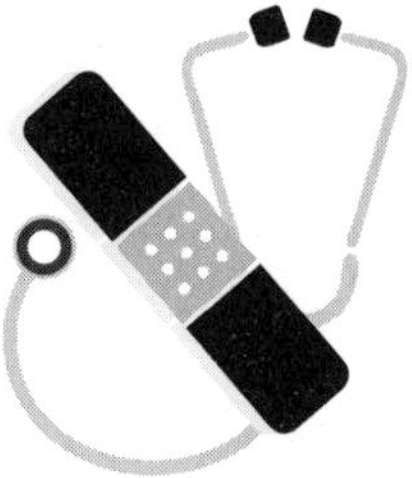

It sure seemed adorable back in the '80s when 16-year-old Doogie Howser, MD, treated his patients. It's less adorable when the teenage doctor is in real life and isn't so much a boy genius as he is a con artist.

Matthew Scheidt was arrested in September 2011 after police said he impersonated a physician's assistant at Osceola Regional Medical Center in Kissimmee, Florida. The 17-year-old went so far as donning scrubs and carrying a stethoscope around his neck.

Although he claimed he was simply given the wrong ID in error, witnesses confirmed Scheidt actually conferred with patients and used his stethoscope to (literally) play doctor. He also managed to interview patients, read through their confidential medical records, perform physical exams, clean wounds, and perform CPR.

When caught, Scheidt had a perfect excuse—he claimed to be an undercover deputy sheriff working on a top-secret investigation. You'd think that would throw authorities off the scent, but he ended up arrested anyway. Four months later, he was caught impersonating a sheriff in Miami Beach, driving through town in what looked suspiciously like a police car.

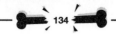

THERE'S A (CORPSE) RIOT GOIN' ON

Back in the eighteenth century, procuring a human body for medical research wasn't an easy task. Such practices were considered taboo, and medical students and doctors, desperate for corpses that could help them learn more about how the human body works, had no other choice but to resort to grave-robbing. They preferred to call themselves "resurrectionists."

In the years following the American Revolution, medical students at New York City's Columbia University routinely raided two nearby cemeteries for deceased paupers and slaves during the winter months. Why winter? Corpses weren't embalmed at the time, so bodies buried during the cold months—and kept fresh by the cold ground—were prime targets. Medical grave-robbing was so common that New York families that could afford it paid guards to protect the graves of their recently deceased loved ones…until enough time passed that the bodies would have decomposed to the point of being useless for medical study.

In February 1788, a group of freed slaves spotted some Columbia students exhuming bodies and signed a petition urging city officials to stop them. Their pleas were ignored, and the resurrectionists continued the ghoulish raids. But on April 13, another student named John Hicks Jr. made a grave mistake. While examining an arm in a dissection room at New

York Hospital, he decided to play a nasty prank on a group of children playing outside. He grabbed the arm and waved it out the window before telling a boy that it belonged to his mother…who actually had just died. Then Hicks threatened to smack him with it.

Traumatized, the boy rushed home to tell his father what had just happened. Furious, the man rushed to his wife's grave in the pauper's cemetery. There he discovered that her body was missing, likely taken by resurrectionists who hadn't even bothered to cover up her empty coffin with dirt (it could, feasibly, actually have been Hicks who'd done it). He quickly assembled a group of friends and neighbors who marched to the hospital in search of Hicks. The growing crowd outside its doors quickly became an angry mob.

They barged in and found bodies in various stages of grisly dissection, while most of the hospital's staff fled in terror, including Hicks. Disgusted and filled with rage, the mob settled for another doctor and three students instead. They dragged them out into the street, but New York mayor James Duane arrived before things really got out of hand. Duane told the mob that he was going to haul the doctor and the students to a jailhouse where they would await trial for their alleged crimes against humanity (and be safe from lynching). The crowd followed them, and by the time the doctor and students were incarcerated, their numbers had reached 2,000 strong. With the subjects of their ire now behind bars, the still-angry mob went in search of new targets.

News of the "horrors" seen in the hospital spread across Manhattan, and thousands of angry citizens took to the streets. That night, no doctor in New York City was safe from the wrath of roaming bands of rioters. Many feared for their lives as a large mob stormed up Broadway calling for the head of John Hicks. One group searched for and failed to find him in the home of a prominent physician... but they neglected to search the attic, where Hicks was hiding.

The riots continued into the next day. New York governor George Clinton called in militia to restore order while the city's doctors fled Manhattan. Another mob set its sights on Columbia University, where they stormed the halls and destroyed various tools and specimens.

Friedrich Wilhelm von Steuben, a Revolutionary War general, led the militia but refused to use force against the mob. After he was hit in the head with a brick, he changed his mind and ordered his men to open fire. Eight rioters were killed by the militia's muskets; many more were wounded. The mobs finally began to disperse, while the city's few remaining doctors, ironically, began tending to the injured.

In the years that followed, New Yorkers remained wary of doctors. Several students were brought to trial for grave-robbing, but Hicks avoided prosecution. In 1789, city officials passed a statute to protect cemeteries and began enforcing strict penalties for resurrectionists. New York's medical schools and hospitals turned to prisons for help in getting bodies for research, but the demand often outweighed the supply.

Desperate, they turned to criminals, typically referred to as "resurrection men," who used the cover of darkness to steal corpses. They often raided cemeteries on Long Island and paid a ferry toll for the "dead drunk friends" they transported back to Manhattan. The practice continued well into the nineteenth century.

✦ ✦ ✦

BONEHEAD

In January 2004, Briana Lane suffered serious head injuries in a car crash near Salt Lake City–so serious that doctors had to remove almost half of her skull to treat the bleeding in her brain. Lane was released in February…but without the missing portion of her skull, which remained behind in the hospital freezer. The skull was due to be replaced, but the day before the surgery, the hospital canceled the appointment: they wanted to wait to see if Medicaid would pay for the procedure. In the meantime, all Lane had over her brain was a flap of skin, and she had to wear a helmet to protect it. (She said that every morning she could feel that her brain had drooped to one side during the night.) Lane finally got her skull back in April–four months after the initial operation. "When you think of weird things happening to people," she said afterward, "you don't think of this."

THE CRANBERRY SOLUTION

In 2003 Trizka Litton of Coventry, England, got some mixed news from her doctor: First, the terrible pain she'd been experiencing indicated she needed a hernia operation. Second, the bad news: The U.K.'s National Health Service treats everyone in the country but is constantly strapped for resources, so Litton was wait-listed until a surgeon was available.

By late 2003, the pain kept getting worse. Seven months on a waiting list was too much for Litton, so she took matters into her own hands. She concocted a cocktail of crumbled biscuits (the British word for "cookies") and cranberry juice, then microwaved it until it formed a thick, gooey, dark red paste. In other words, it looked like blood. Then she called 999 (the British word for "911") and summoned paramedics, claiming she'd vomited blood. She even showed the "blood" to the paramedics, but got rid of it quickly so doctors couldn't test it.

But vomiting blood is enough to move a person way, way up on the hernia operation wait-list. Doctors performed emergency surgery and discovered that her condition had deteriorated: Her stomach was pressing dangerously on her heart. Litton later said her "guilt and shame at being forced to cheat and lie" vanished when doctors realized how close to death she'd been.

SECRET NURSE JARGON

Lantern test. A fictional test a nurse will say she conducted. It means that if she shined a light into a patient's mouth, his whole head would light up, like a lantern, implying that he has no brain and that he's stupid.

N.P.S. "New parent syndrome," the inclination of first-time parents to bring their babies to the hospital for every sniffle and bump.

B.O.N.I.T.A. A nursing acronym that means a patient is about to receive a "big ol' needle in the a**."

M.D. A derisive way nurses refer to pompous doctors. In this instance, the M.D. doesn't stand for "medical doctor" but rather "makes decisions."

R.N. Conversely, some nurses like to think that the R.N. in their job title doesn't stand for "registered nurse" as much as it does "refuses nonsense."

Bloodsuckers. Laboratory technicians–they take blood samples.

Jack-in-the-box. A patient who tries to stand up or walk, even though he can't, and who wobbles around.

Band-Aid Hospital. One of those ubiquitous walk-in, storefront urgent-care clinics.

V.I.P.: A "very intoxicated patient."

7 BEVERAGES MARKETED AS MEDICINE

Coca-Cola, as is widely known, once contained traces of cocaine. Unsurprisingly, it was marketed for its power to "invigorate."

7-Up was also once promoted as a pick-me-up. Until 1950, the formula contained a small amount of lithium, a mood stabilizer long used in the treatment of manic depression, now called bipolar disorder.

Pepsi was marketed as a digestive aid. The original formula contained pepsin, still used today (as in Pepto-Bismol) to soothe upset stomachs.

Angostura Bitters isn't just good for cocktails. It was developed by the surgeon general of Venezuela in 1824, and touted as a cure for hiccups.

Tonic water contains quinine, which is an effective treatment for malaria.

Moxie, the odd-tasting brewed soda loved in New England (and nowhere else) had its origins as a "nerve food." Its creator claimed that it could treat, among other things, "softening of the brain"–a coded reference to syphilis.

Hires Root Beer ads emphasized the medicinal properties of its sassafras oil, a supposed mood booster. Sassafras oil was later banned by the FDA because it contains chemicals toxic to the liver.

GREAT MOMENTS IN TREPANATION, OR DRILLING INTO PEOPLE'S HEADS

5000 BC: During the Neolithic era, the oldest known trepanned human skull is laid to rest at Ensisheim, France.

400 BC: Hippocrates, the "father of medicine," prescribes trepanation to relieve swelling of the brain.

AD 1500: Trepanation flourishes among the Paracas Indians of Peru. Of 10,000 bodies later found in a necropolis near Lima, about 6 percent had been trepanned.

1575 : Belgian inventor Matthia Narvatio pioneers mechanical trepanation, designing a cogwheel rig, similar to a modern hand drill, which drove a circular saw to cut through the skull.

1867: American diplomat Ephraim George Squier, stationed in Peru, uncovers evidence of advanced surgical trepanning among the ancient Incans. Leading anthropologist Paul Broca examines Squier's find and pronounces it genuine. The scientific establishment goes wild.

1965: Dutchman Bart Hughes—unsatisfied with the high from all the mescaline he's been taking—bores a hole in his own skull with an electric drill, hoping to achieve a higher state of consciousness (or something), and so kicks off an underground wave of "recreational" trepanations.

AMOEBAS ATE MY BRAIN!

In September 2013, doctors announced that a 12-year-old Arkansas girl had become just the second American in half a century to survive a bout of *primary amebic meningoencephalitis* (PAM). The disease's name is a mouthful, but it's caused by an amoeba that usually enters the body through the nose. Though the amoeba can lurk in an irrigated garden or a town's water supply, it usually makes contact while a person is swimming in fresh water: a stream, a lake, or even, in Kali Hardig's case, a poorly chlorinated swimming pool.

Once inside the body, the parasite, identified as *naegleria fowleri*, attacks the brain, destroying tissue and causing swelling, headaches, and vomiting. The disease progresses quickly, resulting in confusion, hallucinations, and seizures. Death comes within 7 to 14 days, and it almost always does come. Of 128 reported cases in the U.S. since 1962, researchers identified just one other survivor before Hardig.

The lucky girl overcame the parasite after doctors experimented with a breast-cancer drug. Still, it had done enough damage that Hardig needed to re-learn how to speak, walk, and eat before returning to school.

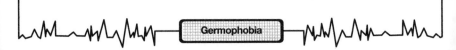

CARVIN' DANA

True or false? Once a standout on *Saturday Night Live* and a big-screen star of the *Wayne's World* films, Dana Carvey's career stalled because of his critically panned 2002 comedy *The Master of Disguise*. Sadly, it's false. Carvey spent a few years in the late '90s suffering not just from heart disease but from the aftereffects of a botched heart surgery.

Carvey first reported heart problems in 1997, and after three angioplasties within a year, he underwent a double-bypass operation in 1998. After the bypass, his chest pain continued. A fourth emergency angioplasty revealed the mistake–his heart surgeon, who had reportedly conducted more than 30,000 similar surgeries, had bypassed the wrong artery. Rather than attaching a healthy segment of artery to the damaged section, the doctor instead attached it to another, nearby healthy section. It took additional surgeries to correct the issues; Carvey spent more than six months incredibly weakened and unable to perform.

After that ordeal, you'd expect Carvey to demand massive restitution, but he claimed he only wanted an apology from the original doctor. Unfortunately, it took him two years and a malpractice lawsuit to get any resolution. Carvey was awarded a $7.5 million judgment against the doctor who performed the botched surgery. He donated all the money to charity.

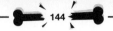

THE JOKES ABOUT HOSPITAL FOOD ARE TRUE

In May 2002, as many as 18 employees at the Hospital of Mollet in Spain reported symptoms associated with food poisoning. It was discovered that all had come down with a case of viral gastroenteritis. A later investigation found that 40 people in all had contracted the infection, which was traced back to a food handler with gastroenteritis working in the hospital's cafeteria.

• In September 1989, there were 84 people hospitalized after they ate in the hospital cafeteria at Jordan University Hospital in Amman, Jordan. Amazingly, the outbreak occurred in the midst of an academic study of the hospital cafeteria to see if the threat of impending "routine surveillance cultures of kitchen employees" would have any effect on food poisoning incidents. "Routine surveillance cultures" is a brainy way of saying "they took routine stool samples of the workers to check for communicable diseases." The study found that most of the individuals who fell ill had eaten mashed potatoes; salmonella was found in the stool of the worker dispensing mashed potatoes.

• A massive wave of hospital-based food poisoning struck Scott from 1973 to 1977. More than 1,530 people became ill after consuming food at 33 hospitals, comprising 50 individual outbreaks. Of those 50, 31 involved the consumption of *Clostridium perfingens*, 11 involved salmonella, and three were from staphylococcus bacteria. Half of the outbreaks took place in geriatric and psychiatric wards.

• There was a nasty run of salmonella at Miriam Hospital in Providence, Rhode Island, in 1987. In all, 27 employees experienced diarrhea and cramping. Of them, 96 percent had eaten in their hospital cafeteria on July 11 or 12, 1987. Fifty other employees were located who had eaten that day who hadn't gotten sick. The difference? The people who got sick were the ones who had tried to be healthy–they'd had salad.

SURGERY ON THE FLY

They're universally agreed upon to be disgusting, but for centuries, fly larvae—*maggots*—have served vital medical functions. They're almost as good at making a meal out of a dead animal as they are at cleaning wounds and preventing infection.

Here comes the science: Maggots feed only on dead organic matter, and powerful enzymes in a maggot's gut kill bacteria and viral pathogens. This makes them uniquely adapted to aid in *debridement*—the cleaning away of dead tissue from wounded or infected areas to better encourage healing.

Evidence suggests that "maggot therapy" has existed for at least a thousand years. Mayan healers were definitely proponents, as were aboriginal healers in Australia. Sixteenth-century French surgeon Ambroise Paré was the first doctor to fully investigate the practice and write about its beneficial effects. At first, like most doctors of his era, he considered maggots destructive and more likely to cause infection than prevent it. While treating a patient for a large head wound, Paré was taken aback when a few crawled out of the man's skull. After pulling himself together, the surgeon noted that the maggots hadn't torn into the delicious, fleshy brain. Instead, they'd eaten only decaying flesh, and the patient remarkably recovered from his injury.

In the decades that followed, maggot therapy was commonly used by field surgeons during military conflicts, especially during the Civil War. But it never caught on in hospitals, where doctors had decidedly less icky tools and resources at their disposal.

It remained a fringe therapy until World War I, when many overwhelmed doctors on the battlefronts of Europe resorted to maggots. After treating a horribly injured soldier who had his life saved by "thousands and thousands of maggots" munching on his wounds, Dr. William S. Baer became an advocate. He conducted a study at Johns Hopkins University and published his findings in 1931. As a result, the therapy caught on among American doctors. A pharmaceutical company even began selling bottles of "Surgical Maggots."

Hundreds of American patients received the therapy throughout the 1930s, but its popularity subsided due to the increasing usage of the far less stomach-churning–and more precise–penicillin in the 1940s. Nevertheless, many imprisoned field surgeons without other options used maggots while treating injured soldiers in Japanese POW camps during World War II. Postwar, maggot therapy died out for decades but was revived in the 1980s by a new generation of advocates. Dozens of studies have since been conducted, arguing that maggot therapy is one of the most effective ways to save a severely injured limb. In 2004, the FDA officially approved maggots for medicinal purposes.

CANADIAN FAKIN'

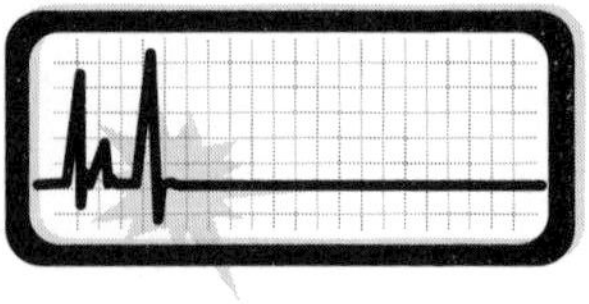

In 1980 the remote, sparsely populated (about 500 people) community of Alert Bay, British Columbia, had a doctor shortage. The town's only doctor, Jack Pickup, had been found negligent in a patient's death. The governing B.C. College of Physicians and Surgeons deemed him competent enough to continue practicing, so long as he had another doctor around to help out.

A call for a new doctor was put out, and only one man was interested in working in Alert Bay: Dr. Robert Rifleman. But after just a few weeks Dr. Pickup found his new colleague to be somewhat incompetent, unable to perform basic exams and other tasks. He asked for the B.C. College of Physicians and Surgeons to do a background check on Rifleman… which they probably should have conducted *before* they hired him.

The organization located Dr. Rifleman—or at least they found a doctor by that name working in Stevens Point, Wisconsin. This Dr. Rifleman quickly cleared up the confusion: On a trip to Mexico in 1978, Dr. Rifleman (the legitimate one) met a doctor named Robert Falcon, who convinced him to volunteer at a clinic. Like Pickup, Rifleman noticed that Falcon didn't really do things by the book (or competently), and questioned if he was really a doctor.

The next day Falcon disappeared, along with Rifleman's diploma, medical license, and birth certificate. That was as close to being a licensed doctor as he'd ever been, or ever would be.

So who was Dr. Rifleman, née Dr. Falcon? Robert Trujillo. A criminal investigation revealed that he had been impersonating doctors for a lot longer than two years.

• In the 1970s, as "Dr. Amos Handel," he'd treated mentally ill children at a government-run group home in Illinois. Around the same time, he'd taught clinical psychology at Elgin Community College, just outside of Chicago.

• Before that, he worked in New York City under the name "Dr. Kevin Michael Murphy" as a child psychiatrist.

• And just before that, he was a common criminal. From 1962 to 1964, he served time for an armed robbery. In 1966 he served six months for stealing an air compressor.

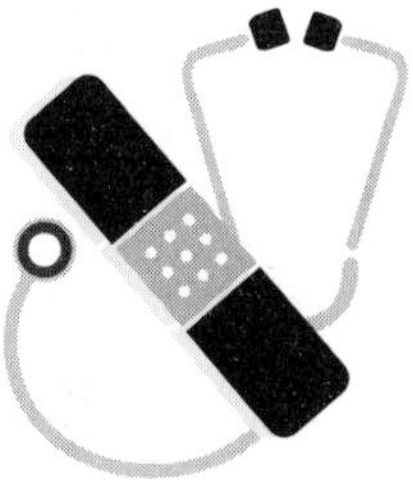

After he was arrested on charges of impersonating a doctor, Trujillo killed himself in prison.

TRUMANCARE

President Obama's Affordable Health Care Act, also known as "Obamacare," isn't the first time a presidential plan to provide all Americans with health insurance has come along.

Harry Truman had been president for only seven months in November 1945, taking over for the deceased Franklin Roosevelt. He planned to pick up where Roosevelt had left off on social welfare. While the New Deal had helped pull the country out of the Depression, one aspect, first proposed in 1938, had failed to be enacted: a national health insurance program.

Truman sent a special letter to Congress, outlining a five-point plan to improve health care in the U.S. "The health of American children, like their education," Truman wrote, "should be recognized as a public responsibility." The points Truman wished to address:

1. Federal funding to increase the number of doctors, dentists, and nurses in underserved rural and low-income areas.

2. Federal funding to build new hospitals in poor and rural counties. According to Truman, 15 million people in the U.S. had either no local hospital or a subpar one.

3. Federal funding to form a board of doctors and public officials to create national standards for hospitals and clinics.

4. The creation of a national health insurance plan. Open to all Americans, but optional, subscribers would pay a monthly fee to the government-run plan, which would cover the coast of any and all medical expenses. Doctors who agreed to treat patients with the national health plan would be paid directly by the government.

5. Subscribers to the national plan would receive wages lost due to illness or injury.

Truman wanted everyone in America to have access to health insurance, particularly the wounded coming home from World War II, those not physically fit enough to serve in World War II, and the destitute helped by Roosevelt's social programs. It was not, nor was it intended to be, government-funded health care. A national poll conducted after Truman's letter to Congress found that 58 percent of the country supported the initiatives.

The legislation reached Congress as a bill to expand Social Security. It was cosponsored by Senator Robert Wagner (D-New York), Senator James Murray (D-Montana), and Representative John Dingell (D-Michigan). Because of their involvement, the legislation became known as the W-M-D Bill. Congressional hearings began in 1946, at which Senator Murray respectfully asked the Republican opposition to refrain from referring to the Truman plan as "socialistic" or "communistic." After all, the Red Scare was underway, and Americans were terrified of the "red menace" of the communist Soviet Union. But Murray need not have worried–Republicans boycotted the hearings. Outside of the chambers of Congress, they were free to call it "socialistic" and "communistic," which is exactly what staunch anti–New Deal senator Robert Taft called it in the press.

The W-M-D Bill was tabled, and in the midterm elections of 1946, Republicans took control of Congress. Wagner was replaced on the Committee on Labor and Public Welfare by, of all people, Taft. Under his direction, a subcommittee discredited the Truman plan by concluding that "known Communists are at work diligently with Federal funds in furtherance of the Moscow party line." In other words, Taft claimed that the national health plan was a plan by Soviet Russia to infiltrate and destroy America. The bill was again tabled.

Undeterred, Truman made the national health plan a cornerstone of his 1948 reelection campaign, which prognosticators widely predicted he'd lose to Republican challenger Thomas Dewey. But Truman unexpectedly won reelection, and that had his opponents running scared–including both congressional Republicans… and doctors. Doctors feared overwork and underpay for having to suddenly treat every person in the United States.

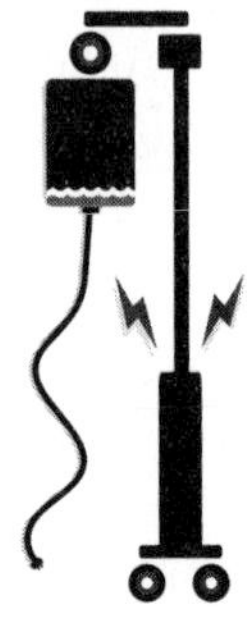

Two major medical organizations publicly opposed Truman's plan: the National Physicians Committee and the American Medical Association. The AMA charged each of its members $25 and gave the money to public relations firm Whitaker and Baxter to mount a massive campaign to destroy the Truman initiatives for good.

The plan included public speakers, radio advertisements, and leaflets, all with the same message: Truman's plan was nothing short of Communism. One pamphlet asked, "Would socialized medicine lead to socialization of other phases of life? Lenin thought so. He declared socialized medicine 'the keystone to the arch of the Socialist State.'" Vladimir Lenin, a Russian revolutionary and architect of the Soviet Union, never said that. Also particularly damning was that the health plan was never referred to as a "health plan"–all the pamphlets, speakers, and advertisements always called the subject "socialized medicine." Its very name linked it to the ideology of the enemy; the Truman plan was doomed.

In 1949, Whitaker and Baxter spent $1.5 million ($14 million in today's money) on its campaign against a national health care plan, the most expensive lobbying effort in American history (to that point). And it worked–a poll in late 1949 found that support for the national health plan had fallen from 58 percent to 36 percent. The bill ultimately died in committee, never reaching a full Congressional vote. Any development on the issue was abandoned in 1950 when the U.S. entered the Korean War...to fight communists.

BLUE IN THE FACE

One late-winter day, a man described in reports as a "43-year-old male" came into Dr. Meyer Schwartz's clinic in Augusta, Georgia, presenting discoloration of the face. As Dr. Schwartz described in a 1987 letter to the *Journal of the American Medical Association*, the lower part of the man's face had turned blue, and the patient said it had been that way for about an hour before he sought treatment. It was a diagnostic puzzle.

With preliminary examination, Dr. Schwartz ruled out hypoxia and cyanosis, both of which cause blue skin due to a lack of properly oxygenated blood or tissue. A thorough medical history discounted trauma, heart disease, or a bleeding disorder. There was no indication of exposure to metallic chemicals, which can cause skin discoloration. And strangely, the effect was strictly localized to the man's face.

Since the patient reported no discomfort or difficulty breathing, and exhibited no neurological impairment, Dr. Schwartz deemed him to be in no immediate danger. He was discharged, pending a full toxicology workup. Soon afterward, the man called the clinic and apologetically told Dr. Schwartz to cancel the follow-up. The tint turned out to be the residue from a new set of blue towels he'd received for Christmas. The coloring disappeared when the patient…washed his face.

THE PLAGUE

Yersinia pestis is one of history's most destructive diseases. This nasty bug has been given many nicknames over the centuries: the pestilence, the blue sickness, the Black Death, and the bubonic plague. It was so bad, it doesn't even need modifiers–it's best known as, simply, "the plague."

Symptoms appear within two to five days after infection. What seems like a bad cold eventually gives way to more severe complaints, like a high fever, muscle cramps, and gangrene. Many victims develop a pink hue to their skin, which eventually turns to full-on rot, along with massively swollen lymph nodes, vomiting, extreme pain, and, if the patient is lucky before they mercifully perish, coma.

The earliest known outbreak of the disease devastated the Byzantine Empire in 541–542. The epidemic was dubbed the "Plague of Justinian," for Emperor Justinian I. He managed to survive, but millions of his countrymen weren't so lucky. The disease initially hit Constantinople, the empire's capital. At the worst period of the outbreak, 10,000 people died every day.

The Plague of Justinian was thought to have originated in Africa. In order to feed the masses of Constantinople, the emperor ordered tons of grain from Egypt. Unfortunately, tons of rats covered in plague-carrying fleas also tagged along on the boats that carried the grain to the capital. As it bombarded

Constantinople, the disease quickly spread across the rest of the empire. It severely weakened Justinian's military and prevented his forces from successfully conquering northern Italy. The initial wave subsided, but the disease returned nearly every generation in the ensuing centuries and spread beyond the empire's borders. The last major recurrence occurred in 750. Before it finally went dormant, the Plague killed more than 50 million people across Africa, Europe, and Asia.

Flash forward to the thirteenth century. As unusually warm temperatures gave way to the Little Ice Age, crops all across Europe began to fail while massive amounts of livestock began to die. As a result, millions went hungry and their immune systems became weakened, paving the way for the plague's big comeback.

This next epidemic, commonly referred to as the Black Death, and the one usually being referred to when "the plague" is mentioned, was enormously destructive. Historians believe that it originated in China and slowly spread across Asia—Mongolian warriors carried the disease to the shores of Italy during an effort to invade Caffa in the fall of 1346. The following spring, the city's population fled via ships to southern Europe to escape the Mongols. And who joined them? Rats—and their fleas carrying *Yersinia pestis*.

The plague blasted north across Europe like an impossibly calamitous wildfire in the six miserable years that followed. Exact numbers are impossible to determine, but it's estimated that during this period, the Black Death killed no fewer than 25 million people and as many as 200 million. Half the population of Paris, Florence, and other major cities were killed.

Fourteenth-century doctors were at a loss to explain the calamity. Many considered the plague the wrath of God or a sign of the apocalypse. Thousands placed the blame on minority groups and lepers. Jews were especially targeted, leading to the full-scale genocide of Jewish communities all across Germany.

As with the Plague of Justinian, the Black Death bounced back every generation or so in the following decades. An epidemic hit Moscow in the 1770s. Despite massive quarantine efforts, the disease brought the city's economy to a near halt, leading to widespread food shortages, which in turn led to a three-day riot in September 1771 by hungry citizens, which then led to the murder-by-mob of Ambrosius, the archbishop of Moscow.

But even with modern medical advances, particularly antibiotics and knowledge about how the disease is spread, the plague isn't ancient history. The plague even hit San Francisco at the turn of the twentieth century. Scientists fear that a drug-resistant strain of *Yersinia pestis* could develop someday...not unlike the one that appeared in Madagascar in 1995.

THOSE "OTHER" PLAGUES

Sure, we've all heard of bubonic plague, (see page 155), but while "the Black Death" may be the flashiest, there have been plenty of other horrible pandemics.

The Spanish Flu

Some estimate the global flu pandemic of 1918 killed more people than bubonic plague, rampaging all corners of the globe and devastating the lives of several characters on *Downton Abbey*. And it did it all in less than two years. Because the disease sparked an overreaction of the immune system, it was actually most lethal in healthy young people. It's estimated the Spanish flu killed anywhere from 50 to 100 million people, around 5 percent of the world's population.

The Early AIDS Epidemic

While AIDS may not have claimed a death toll as high as other epidemics, its mortality rate in the early years was nearly 100 percent. Prior to 1981, fewer than 100 cases were reported in the U.S. Ten years later, the number was nearly 60,000. The spread of the disease coupled with its high mortality rate made AIDS the leading cause of death among Americans ages 25 to 44 by 1994. Since then, improved treatment and prevention methods have decreased both the mortality rate and the pace of new infections.

Smallpox, or the "American Plague"

When Europeans first arrived on the shores of the Americas, they brought with them a grab bag of diseases to which the native people had never been exposed, most notably smallpox. The disease spread across the continent faster than European migration, so written census records often began after a population had been decimated. It's estimated the death toll was in the millions, in some areas wiping out up to 90 percent of the population. But it was also a two-way street: Native Americans introduced a virulent strain of syphilis that soon spread across western Europe.

Typhus

Typhus is caused by a bacteria, carried by lice and fleas who live on mice and rats, which then can infect humans. Symptoms include high fever, severe body pain, vomiting, and delirium. (That's why it's called typhus–*typhos* is a Greek word that means "hazy.") Typhus was likely the disease behind the Plague of Athens, which ravaged the city during the Peloponnesian War in 430 B.C. But the most devastating outbreak occurred during and after World War I. More than 25 million people in Russia were infected, and four million in Poland. Delousing stations for troops helped, but as many as 40 percent of infected soldiers still died, as did the nurses attending to them. Vaccines were developed after World War II (during which time the disease spread through battlefields and concentration camps), but outbreaks still occur today, primarily in homeless encampments and refugee centers.

DIAGNOSIS HUH?

Along with his wife Tracey Thorn, Ben Watt comprised the pop duo Everything But the Girl. Hugely popular in England, they had one massive hit in the U.S.: "Missing" in 1995. At the peak of the band's European success in 1992, Watt fell ill with excruciating stomach pain and checked into a hospital. The first doctor thought he was having a heart attack, as severe abdominal pain is indicative of either a long, slow heart attack or a short, intense one. Other doctors thought that, because Watt was a rock musician, the sickness was drug-related, even though he claimed not to be a drug user.

Watt was shuffled around from doctor to doctor, ward to ward, his symptoms growing worse and varied. The stomach pain got even worse, accompanied by a temperature of 105, vomiting, and an inability to swallow or eat, move his hands, speak, or turn onto his side. This went on for nine weeks, as his doctors were stymied.

After undergoing dozens of clinical tests and after he'd lost 46 pounds, Watt's condition was finally diagnosed: Churg-Strauss syndrome. It's an extremely rare autoimmune disease. How rare? Only 25 people have been diagnosed with it in the past 40 years.

Doctors didn't think of it sooner—not because of its novelty but because of the way Watt's symptoms developed: Churg-Strauss generally affects the lungs first, not the stomach.

Because the disease went untreated for so long, Watt suffered irreversible harm. First, 10 feet of his small intestine—which is only 13 feet long to begin with—had been completely destroyed by antibodies and a blocked blood supply, creating necrosis, or tissue death. Those 10 feet of dead intestine had to be removed and the two ends of his intestine surgically reconnected.

Having three feet of intestines severely limits Watt's digestive system, of course. Since 1992 he's been on a permanent, restrictive diet. He can eat, more or less, hand-size meals consisting primarily of chicken, rice, white bread, and lettuce. Watt has been able to gain back only 13 of the 46 pounds he lost during his nightmarish nine-week hospital stay. He takes a daily cocktail of medicines and sports a surgical scar running from his torso down to his legs.

But he lived.

✚ ✚ ✚

SPIRITED TREATMENT

Kohinoor Bibi and Makid Mandal charged patients in a rural Indian village $60 to treat conditions including appendicitis, gallstones, and hernias. But they weren't doctors—they merely claimed to channel "ghost doctors." They amassed a small fortune in their three-month run in 2005 as "healers"...before they were arrested.

THE BAD DR. KING

William Henry King grew up poor in mid-1800s Ontario, but became a doctor after his marriage to Sarah Lawson in 1855–her wealthy father picked up his medical school bill. The future seemed wife open for the newlyweds...until the church-going, curse-word-averse King let his true nature show after the birth of his first child.

The daughter was born handicapped, and died after a month. Sarah suspected King, who had started to abuse her, of killing the baby outright, and fled to her parents' house. King, unfazed, continued working toward his degree and graduated with top honors from Pennsylvania Medical University. He returned to Canada in 1858, and, amazingly, managed to win back Sarah. King threw himself into building a successful medical practice...as well as into an affair with a woman named Melinda Vandervoort.

The two exchanged syrupy letters behind Sarah's back. William told Melinda that Sarah was ill and would soon die, implying that the two of them could be together once she was out of the way. Strangely enough, Sarah soon came down with a sudden case of what her not-at-all-suspicious doctor husband called "cholera." King treated her himself and prescribed a powdered white medicine. Within a month, Sarah Lawson was dead.

King put on a good show at her funeral, pretending to be overwhelmed with grief, but Sarah's family didn't fall for it. Rumors swirled around Hamilton and beyond about the doctor and Melinda Vandervoort. Sarah's father organized an investigation into her mysterious death, and King panicked. He fled with Vandervoort, hiding out at a farm in New York until authorities tracked them down and dragged them back to Hamilton.

The ensuing murder trial in the spring of 1859 was a sensation that captured headlines all over Canada for reasons beyond the grisly details. For the first time in the country's history, the judge had allowed forensic evidence to be used by the prosecutor. A professor from Toronto testified, revealing that he had discovered 11 grams of deadly arsenic in Sarah's stomach. That would be the mysterious white powdered medicine King had given her.

That was about all it took for the jury to convict King. In what would become Ontario's last public hanging, the cruel doctor was trotted out in front of 10,000 spectators the following June. His execution was practically a public holiday. Nearby Victoria College closed for the day so its students and faculty could attend. Before his noose was tightened, King finally confessed to the crowd and talked about his faith. He went to his grave believing that God had forgiven him for his crime.

BRING BACK THE SPARK

There's a wearying progression in the history of quack medicine from science to pseudoscience. New fields of legitimate scientific inquiry open up, only to be co-opted by a parade of cranks and grifters. So it was even with electricity. At the turn of the twentieth century, as more homes were first wired into the grid, consumers were actively seeking appliances to plug into their brand-new wall sockets—and the legions of medical fraudulence rushed to fill that void, peddling arcs and sparks as the latest miracle cure.

In *cranial electrotherapy stimulation*—developed in 1902—a "gentle" current pulsed over the skull by means of electrodes attached to the scalp, eyelids, or earlobes. Supposedly, this could relieve anxiety and insomnia, and even ease narcotic withdrawal, perhaps by boosting serotonin levels. Shockingly (pun intended), CES is still in use today as an alternative therapy, despite scant evidence as to its effectiveness.

Rather more worrying is the "galvanic bath." This procedure sees patients reclining in a hot tub while low-amperage currents pass through the water, allegedly relieving inflammation of the joints. Higher-amperage currents would, of course, relieve you of life itself, which is why your mom warned you not to bring the radio into the bathroom.

THIS WILL SHOCK YOU

Shock therapy is intended to cure insanity. So if you're insane enough to do it on yourself, it should be especially effective, right? It will come as no surprise to the sane among you that, no, electrocuting your brain by yourself isn't a good idea.

Electroshock therapy, or electroconvulsive therapy (ECT), as it's diplomatically called, is the procedure of sending a short extremely controlled burst of electric current directly into the brain. Surprisingly, this stuff of *Frankenstein* and mid-century mental-ward horror is, today, an increasingly accepted treatment for schizophrenia and other mental illnesses. That doesn't apply to "self-administered shock therapy", or attaching your head to a car battery, as it's diplomatically called.

Like setting yourself on fire, sitting in a homemade electric chair seems like a torture no one would invite. But research in the *Journal of ECT* says it's an increasingly common phenomenon. According to one report, multiple patients followed instructions from an online manual to shock themselves. The result was scorched temples and skin grafts, but "no proper psychopathological improvement."

TRAINING REGIMEN

It seems as if silent-movie villains have been getting a bad rap all along. All those times they tied damsels in distress to train tracks? Turns out they were just trying to cure them of various maladies. At least that's probably what a devoted cabal of people in Indonesia might think.

Convinced that mainstream health-care practices are not up to the task of improving their health, many Indonesians have started riding the rails, literally. They lie across the tracks, touching their hands and feet to the electrically wired rails, and wait for that sweet jolt of healthy electricity to course through their bodies. Not even the threat of fines, jail time, or sudden death can stop them.

While the curative effects of unregulated electricity are debatable at best, seeing dozens of people doing the shimmy on railroad tracks sure makes for an interesting spectacle. If it turns out that this self-electric shock therapy works, we can expect a lot of copycats. A word of advice before you rush out for some Amtrak therapy, however: We recommend starting slowly, maybe by licking a battery or something similar.

On second thought, just don't.

NO DAY BUT TODAY

Many of history's great artists never received the recognition they deserved while they were still alive. For Jonathan Larson, the composer and author of the hit musical *Rent*, his pre-fame death was particularly cruel and ill-timed.

Larson used his experience living in grimy 1980s New York City to write *Rent,* a musical about troubled bohemian artists living in a rundown Alphabet City apartment building, many of them dying from AIDS. It took Larson years to write it and get it produced; he worked as a waiter in a diner for a decade to pay his bills.

In the week prior to opening night, Larson began complaining of chest pains and nausea, but the doctors chalked it up to the stress of opening a Broadway show. A few days later, in the early morning of January 25, 1996, Larson collapsed just hours before the first preview performance of *Rent.* An autopsy would later declare that Larson died of an aortic dissection caused by undiagnosed Marfan syndrome.

A musical about the fleeting quality of life (and whose advertising tagline was "no today but today") took on extra poignancy. Doctors failing to notice Larson's ailment meant Larson didn't get to enjoy the payoff of his long starving artist period–*Rent* won a Tony Award for Best Musical and a Pulitzer Prize.

THOSE FERTILE FORTIES

The idea that women in their late 30s are less likely to get pregnant than women in their late 20s is a myth. It was debunked in 2013 by Jean Twenge, a psychology professor at San Diego State University.

• The American Society for Reproductive Medicine states in its guidelines that women ages 35 to 39 have a 30 percent chance of not conceiving after a year of trying. The data is from a 2004 article in the journal *Human Reproduction*.

• Another widely reported statistic: Women age 40 and over have a 5 percent chance of getting pregnant.

The source of the data for both of those stats: data collected in France...between 1670 and 1830. That's woefully outdated information from before antibiotics and modern medical advancements that have increased the quality of life and the average lifespan of the human race, particularly for women.

To counter this data, Twenge cites an article in *Obstetrics and Gynecology*. In 2004 a study of 770 European women found that 82 percent of women ages 35 to 39 conceived within a year of trying... versus a marginally more 86 percent of women ages 27 to 34. Twenge says that actual medical problems, such as endometriosis or blocked fallopian tubes, are far more to blame for infertility–not simply age.

NO MSG

Myth: Consumption of MSG-laden Chinese food can lead to headaches, flushing, swelling, and chest pain.

Truth: Developed in 1908 by Japanese food scientists, MSG, short for monosodium glutamate, is a flavor enhancer. It makes foods taste savory and stimulates the appetite. Sold in crystalline form, it's widely used by Asian restaurants in the United States.

Thousands of people claim to have an MSG allergy or sensitivity, ever since the rise in popularity of Chinese food in the 1950s. It wasn't the authentic Chinese food, but heavy Western dishes like General Tso's chicken and sweet-and-sour pork that led to a phenomenon called "Chinese Restaurant Syndrome," characterized by facial flushing, swelling, and headaches. MSG, an exotic ingredient in this new exotic cuisine, was believed to be the culprit.

Here's the kicker: Chinese Restaurant Syndrome isn't real. In fact, no study has ever conclusively linked CRS symptoms with MSG. So why do people get nasty headaches and turn bright red after a big Chinese meal? Because they just ate a big Chinese meal. MSG is an appetite stimulant, so diners eat more than they otherwise would have, and it's high-calorie, heavily salted food, packed with a generous wallop of sugar. Simply put, people feel bad after eating Chinese food because this kind of Chinese food is unhealthy.

A LOT OF LOBOTOMIES

Of all the surgical absurdities inflicted on humans through the centuries, few have been designed and performed with such missionary zeal—and with such frequently disastrous consequences—as the lobotomy. Seen as an attempt to lessen the suffering of the mentally afflicted by severing neural connections to and from the brain's prefrontal cortex, lobotomies were performed more than 40,000 times in the United States and more than 20,000 times in Europe during their heyday in the mid-twentieth century.

Eventually, lobotomies would be described as "frontal-lobe castration" by author Ken Kesey in his psych-ward novel *One Flew Over the Cuckoo's Nest*. Tales of patients whose minds had been thoroughly scrambled by the procedure—combined with the advent of effective medications—have rendered the procedure largely obsolete. But for years, lobotomies were considered a breakthrough in the treatment of schizophrenia, "mental retardation," and other brain disorders.

At first, the procedure's European pioneers (most prominently the Portuguese neurologist António Egas Moniz, who won the Nobel Prize for his efforts) performed it exclusively in operating rooms under general anesthesia and in sanitary conditions. But once neuropsychiatrist Walter Freeman had imported the lobotomy to the U.S., he realized that because most mental institutions lacked adequate surgical facilities, some simplification would be required if the procedure were to reach its full therapeutic potential.

So Freeman began experimenting in his kitchen with an ice pick and a grapefruit, and by 1946 he had performed the first "transorbital" lobotomy, better known as the "ice-pick lobotomy." It involved peeling back the upper eyelid and forcing a sharp instrument into the brain above the eyeball, then real scientifically swirling the instrument (as one might use an egg-beater) to tear away at the cortex's neural connectors.

Once lobotomies moved from the O.R. to the psychiatrist's office, the number of procedures exploded, from fewer than 700 between 1940 and 1944 to more than 5,000 in 1949 alone.

When the treatment was successful, the neural severing could result in decreased psychosis and increased contentment. Still, the procedure's "success" rate remained perilously low, and horror stories of unsuccessful lobotomies were legion even as the surgery became more prevalent. Tennessee Williams's sister Rose, a paranoid schizophrenic, was left with little of her personality after their mother agreed to have her lobotomized. The playwright, wracked with guilt, used Rose's plight as the inspiration for *The Glass Menagerie* and *Suddenly, Last Summer*. In the former, a nearly catatonic young girl spends all day playing with glass animals; in the latter, a wealthy matriarch forces a lobotomy on her niece.

Both plays were popular and served to raise awareness of the downside of lobotomization—but none quite like the sad case of Rosemary Kennedy, sister of John, Robert, and Ted. She was deemed "slow-witted" as a child (her IQ tested under 70) but was able to keep a diary and engage socially. When she developed violent mood swings as a young adult, her father, Joseph P. Kennedy, agreed to subject Rosemary to a lobotomy in 1941. The doctors, including Freeman, kept her awake during the surgery and asked her to sing and recite the Lord's Prayer while they cut into her frontal lobe; they stopped cutting when she became incoherent. The procedure left her permanently incapacitated and unable to live on her own, though she would survive for more than 60 years in institutions.

Ironically, Dr. Freeman's last patient was also one of the first to go under his ice pick. Helen Mortensen had been one of the initial recipients of a transorbital lobotomy in 1946, then had a second procedure 10 years later. A few years after that, she asked for a third lobotomy, but Freeman severed a blood vessel during the surgery and Mortensen died. Freeman's hospital privileges were revoked, and he retired soon afterward...as did the lobotomy as a common course of treatment.

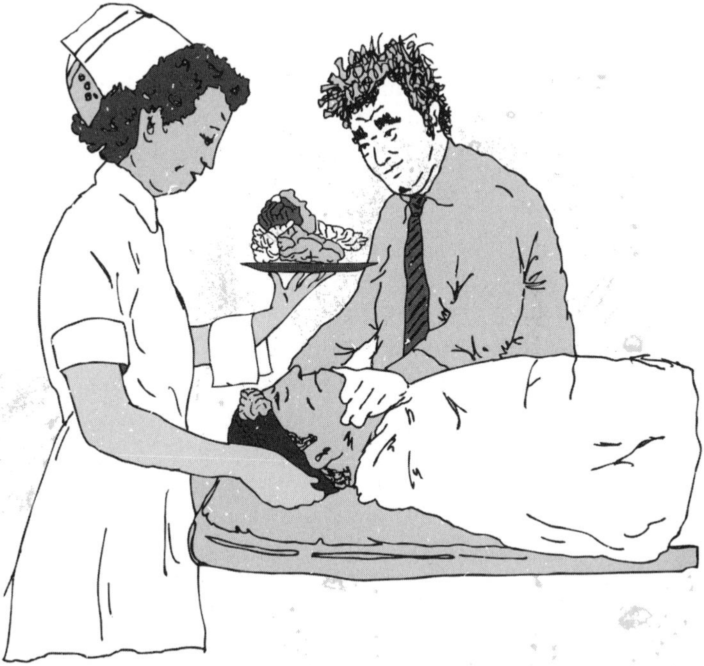

DENTAL DAMN

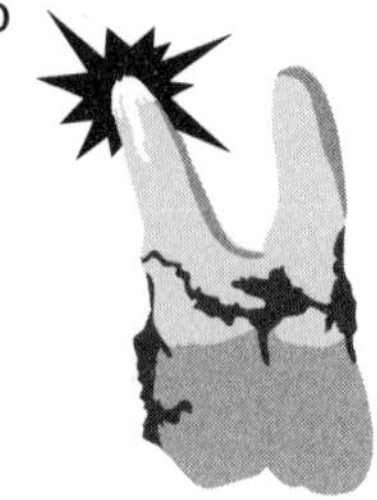

In 2013, Christopher Crist, 21, went to Amazing Family Dental, an Indianapolis dental practice, to have three teeth removed. He went there on the recommendation of his mother, who looks after Crist—he has been diagnosed as falling on the autism spectrum, and as such has trouble communicating and expressing himself.

Crist reportedly showed up at Amazing Family Dental with written instructions from his mother explaining which three teeth were to be removed. The note apparently didn't say to remove only those three teeth, because apparently that's the kind of thing you have to do these days. After the dentist (unnamed in reports) gave Crist a painkiller, he removed the three requested teeth…and continued to pull teeth. He kept going…until all of Crist's teeth were gone.

To make matters worse, Crist developed a nasty infection in his now tooth-free mouth, which required hospitalization. More bad news—an investigation by an Indianapolis TV news crew found that Amazing Family Dental has not-so-amazingly done this before. A former patient named Rose Hill claimed that she once came into the practice with a toothache in one tooth and left without any of her bottom row of teeth.

TOOTH OR DARE

By now you've learned that it's shockingly not unusual for surgeons to leave medical tools inside their patients. What is unusual is for those tools to linger in the human body unnoticed for more than 40 years.

In 1967 Tim Springer, 18, had his wisdom teeth removed. Back then, such a procedure meant an overnight hospital stay and plenty of morphine. Because the teeth were severely impacted, doctors actually pulled them in two operations and removed two of Springer's molars to make room for the impacted wisdom teeth. The surgery went fine, and Springer went on with his life.

About 40 years later, Springer visited his dentist complaining of pain in his jaw. An X-ray revealed the culprit—a small piece of a stainless steel dental instrument had been lodged in his jaw. After confirming that the instrument wasn't placed there by his current dentist, the only logical explanation was that the surgeon who'd removed the wisdom teeth left it behind.

"All I can imagine is a guy sitting on my chest and pulling and pulling with this instrument until the tip cracked off," Springer said. The object in question was just the top of an instrument, only about an eighth of an inch long, but big enough to cause pain. Fortunately, Springer's current dentist was able to remove the item; unfortunately, Springer wasn't allowed to keep the item as a souvenir.

TWINS BENEATH THE SKIN

In most families, the birth of twins is an unusual, even shocking, event. For London's Kelly family, it was business as usual. When their sons were conceived in 1992, mom Alyson already had twins by a previous partner. So did dad Errol. So discovering that Alyson was carrying twins again was not as big a shock as it would have been in another family.

They reacted too soon. When one of their sons was born black, like Errol, and the other white, like Alyson—well, *that* was a shock.

Like most black people who are descended from slaves, Errol—who is Jamaican—carries a dash of European ancestry in his DNA. In biracial children, the genes for African characteristics will usually dominate to a greater or lesser degree, but on rare occasions the recessive European traits will manifest.

And even more rarely (in only one of 500 sets of mixed-race fraternal twins, geneticists estimate), one child will inherit the European DNA while the other will not, leading to twins who share the same family and the same life—but who will always be seen very differently by the world.

SUPERFECUNDATION!

Maybe you've referred to your best friend jokingly as your "twin brother from another mother." That's just a figure of speech, of course. But it is possible–however rare–to have a twin sister from another mister.

Superfecundation differs from ordinary fraternal twinning in that the two eggs are not fertilized at the same time but rather in two separate, but very closely timed, sexual encounters. And occasionally those sexual encounters will be with two different partners. When that happens, it's called *heteropaternal superfecundation*.

Heteropaternal superfecundation is pretty common in the animal kingdom–stray dogs, for instance, will often give birth to litters wherein each pup has a different sire. It's rare in humans, though. How rare, we cannot say for sure, since it is only revealed by DNA testing after the fact. But out of all court-ordered paternity tests where fraternal twins are involved–a sampling that in itself, thankfully, represents only a tiny fraction of the general population–only around 2.5 percent, or one in 40, indicate that the twins have different fathers. This qualifies heteropaternal superfecundation as a genuine miracle of science–albeit a sordid and skeevy one.

BEACHED BOY

Brian Wilson is as well known for his descent into mental illness in the 1970s as he is for writing indelible pop classics like "God Only Knows" and "Wouldn't It Be Nice" for the Beach Boys in the 1960s. By 1975 Wilson's weight had risen to 300 pounds, and he spent most of his time lying in bed due to a drug addiction, alcoholism, and severe depression. His wife, Marilyn Wilson, had had enough and hired a clinical psychologist, Dr. Eugene Landy, she'd seen on TV talk shows. A "shrink to the stars," Landy had treated many celebrities, from Alice Cooper to Rod Steiger, for everything from addiction to depression.

His methods were experimental and tough, and he believed in 24-hour-a-day therapy (which cost a minimum of $35,000 a month). Either Landy or one of his 14 assistants was always with Wilson, doing things like padlocking the refrigerator and pouring buckets of water on Wilson if he refused to get out of bed. Results? Wilson slimmed down, and he started getting out of bed.

While Wilson's health was improving, his wife and Beach Boys bandmates thought Landy's techniques were dangerous and unethical. Landy allegedly isolated Wilson from anyone who disagreed with the treatments, including Marilyn Wilson and his brothers/bandmates, and fed him a large diet of mind-numbing prescription drugs. Landy moved in with Wilson and started charging $2.50 *a minute* for his therapy–plus personal expenses.

Landy so thoroughly took over Wilson's health that in 1983 he began steps to take over Wilson's entire life. In 1983 he became Wilson's manager as well as doctor (an illegal ethics violation). He even co-wrote and produced Brian Wilson's 1988 solo comeback album. Through the urging by Wilson's family, Landy was taken to task by the California Board of Medical Quality, and his license was revoked for many ethical violations.

But no matter. Landy just had more time to focus on Wilson. He formed a production company called Brains and Genius and made Wilson a partner. He even allegedly co-wrote Wilson's Landy-praising memoir *Wouldn't It Be Nice*. (Wilson later admitted that he hadn't even read the book, let alone written it. Nor could he have–Landy kept him isolated and drugged.)

Landy's critical mistake: He had Wilson's will rewritten to make himself the primary beneficiary. That's when Wilson's family stepped in and took the matter to court. In 1992, finally, Landy was barred from all contact with Brian Wilson.

Amazingly, Landy got his license back, and he practiced psychology in New Mexico and Hawaii until his death in 2006. Wilson, while frail at times, has been able to tour and record new albums…thanks to conventional psychiatry.

THE DILLINGER DILEMMA

It's become a familiar movie trope for criminals to change their appearance with plastic surgery to avoid police detection. But with the FBI breathing down his neck, famed bank robber John Dillinger went under the knife for real, and the results were about what you'd expect from backroom plastic surgery in 1934.

Having escaped from prison for the second time, with his mug adorning wanted posters around the country, Dillinger asked his attorney to find a surgeon to alter his face. They eventually found Dr. Wilhelm Loeser, recently paroled after serving time for dealing cocaine and heroin. Loeser operated on Dillinger in a Chicago apartment. The doctor was instructed to remove several identifying marks on Dillinger's face, smooth over his prominent cleft chin, and burn off his fingerprints with acid–a procedure Loeser had invented and performed on himself.

After Dillinger nearly choked on his tongue under general anesthetic, he underwent the remainder of the surgery awake. Loeser cut away several moles and used kangaroo tendons to stretch Dillinger's face. The surgery left Dillinger in pain, his face distorted... but still clearly recognizable. When he was gunned down by FBI agents just two months later outside the Biograph Theater, Dillinger was easily identified by fingerprints and...his famous face.

THE PLASTIC SURGERY ADDICT

Plastic surgery has become so common over the last couple of decades that most people would bat their surgically enhanced eyes at a mall kiosk advertising $20 Botox injections as quickly as they would at other quasi-medical mall-based services, like teeth whitening or optometry. London resident Cindy Jackson is probably the world's foremost beneficiary of the mainstreaming of cosmetic enhancement surgery.

Jackson was first drawn to changing her appearance at age 14, when a stranger in her hometown of Hazard, Kentucky, told her that she had a long nose. These words stuck with Jackson, and after the death of her father, she used her inheritance to get a little work done. That "little work" soon turned into a lifelong project. In 2000, *Guinness World Records* confirmed that she held claim to "most cosmetic surgery procedures to date." The many nips and tucks she's had to her face and body include five facelifts and liposuctions and a total of $100,000 spent on her various procedures.

Jackson has used her plastic surgery expertise to make a living by teaching others how to keep looking young. According to her website, she provides plastic surgery and anti aging consultation and has written two books about the medical sculpting she loves so much.

BAD NEWS, GOOD NEWS

It may seem like a cliché, but sometimes the doctor really does have good news to offset the bad.

The Bad News: You've got herpes.

The Good News: The herpes virus has been shown to be effective in treating several forms of cancer, including an aggressive form of breast cancer that is otherwise resistant to hormone therapies.

The Bad News: You still have herpes.

The Good News: Herpes has been shown to protect against bubonic plague.

The Bad News: Due to a history of bronchitis or living for a long period at a high altitude, you've developed secondary polycythemia. The consistent lack of oxygen in the body leads to overproduction of red blood cells. That means overly thick blood, which can cause blood clots and strokes.

The Good News: All that extra oxygen makes you feel great—because it increases your energy and physical stamina.

The Bad News: You got circumcised.

The Good News: Baby foreskins can be ground up into an ingestible powder, which is used to treat ulcers. Used whole, foreskins can be made into skin grafts for burn victims. Mazel Tov!

The Bad News: You've got hookworms.

The Good News: Research shows that hookworms can alleviate, or even completely eliminate, allergies.

The Bad News: You've got sickle-cell anemia.

The Good News: People who carry the sickle-cell gene experience less severe symptoms when infected with malaria. Granted, that's a benefit only if you also have malaria, but let's focus on the positive here.

The Bad News: You've been exposed to tuberculosis. Okay, you *have* tuberculosis.

The Good News: You are at a reduced risk of developing asthma, so you can breathe easily and focus on the fact that you probably have tuberculosis.

BONE STRETCHING

Bones aren't exactly made for stretching; that's generally the job of muscles and tendons. But for patients with certain medical conditions or bone deformities, a procedure called *distraction osteogenesis*—that's a fancy name for "bone stretching"—is the solution.

Here's how the incredibly painful surgery happens (not for the squeamish): Doctors break the bone, separate it, and then put a spacer (known as a distractor) in the newly created gap. Patients can then turn the distractor very slowly, lengthening the space—and once they achieve a desired or ideal length, bone tissue will automatically grow in the gap and fuse with the existing bones. It's far more effective, and somewhat less painful, than a medieval torture rack.

Bone stretching is suitable for a variety of parts of the body, from the lower or upper jaw to arms and legs. But in rare cases, patients request this procedure not for legitimate medical reasons, but in order to become taller. Examples of this cosmetic bone stretching have occurred in China and, most recently, in Australia, where politician Hajnal Ban gained three inches—and is now 63 inches tall—after her procedure. "I wanted to be taller," she told Reuters. "I'm not embarrassed or ashamed of it. I had an insecurity and the means to fix it."

LET'S KILL PRESIDENT McKINLEY!

After losing his job in the economic depression of 1893, Leon Czolgosz became an anarchist. As such, he came to view the American government, particularly President William McKinley, as oppressors, and believed that they needed to be stopped. In 1901 Czolgosz decided to assassinate McKinley. So he waited for him in a receiving line at the Temple of Music in the Pan-American Exposition. This was before the days of intensive Secret Service protection, so regular citizens really could just stand in a line and wait to meet the president.

Czolgosz met the president on September 6, 1901...and shot him twice. One bullet grazed McKinley, and the other lodged in his abdomen. And that's how Czolgosz assassinated President McKinley. Although he had some accomplices: bad medical decision-making and just plain bad luck.

• McKinley was taken via ambulance across the vast exposition to the festival's "hospital," but it was really just a medical tent. No doctors were present, only some nurses.

• An area doctor named Herman Mynter was summoned, as was Matthew Mann, a gynecologist. Neither had any experience in treating gunshot wounds. They opted to operate to retrieve the bullet from the abdomen of the still-conscious McKinley, giving him morphine for the pain, and to knock him out.

• It was early evening by this point, and the only source of operating light, the sun, was starting to set. To get more light, the doctors had a third person hold a mirror above the operating table, which reflected in a fair-to-poor amount of extra light.

• An electric light was being rigged up. The doctors were about done with the surgery when it was finally ready.

• As it was a medical tent, the facility didn't have much surgical equipment on hand, if any. Mann managed to find a scalpel, so he sliced open McKinley's stomach. Since he had no retractors to hold the wound open or probing tools to probe the wound, Mann held open the wound with one hand and dug around inside the president's abdomen with the other. This incredibly precise method did manage to find the entry wound and what Mann wrongly thought was an exit wound.

• Ironically, Mann could have found the bullet a lot faster and with a lot less transmission of germs from his hand to the president's open wound. An attraction at the exposition was one of the world's first X-ray machines. Mann didn't use it because he thought the contraption would frighten President McKinley.

• Again, lacking basic medical supplies, Mann stitched up the incision and wounds with black silk thread and slapped a bandage on top. Really.

• Oh, and he forgot to clean or drain the wounds.

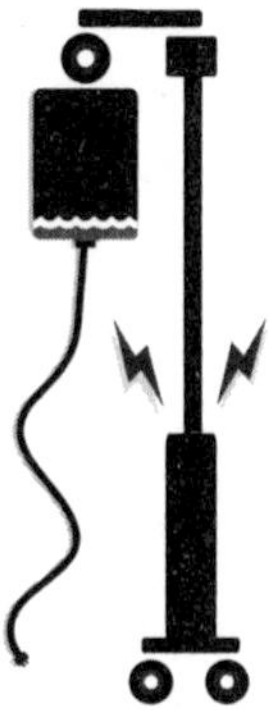

To recover, McKinley was taken to a nearby home called the Milburn House. He woke up the morning of September 7, conscious and in good spirits. For all intents and purposes, it seemed as if McKinley was improbably recovering from 1) being shot in the stomach, and 2) the haphazard surgery thereafter. Vice President Theodore Roosevelt cut short a vacation in Vermont to see McKinley—just in case—as did some cabinet members. All left on September 9 when it looked like McKinley would fully recover.

But he wasn't recovering—he was slowly dying. Czolgosz's bullet traveled through McKinley's stomach, as well as his pancreas and a kidney. That left a trail of gangrene, which grew and spread as the days passed. McKinley was obese, which slowed—but didn't stop—the spread of the deadly infection.

On the morning of September 11, McKinley drank some broth, and the next day was able to keep down toast, coffee, and some more broth. But excruciating stomach pain quickly developed. At this point, was gangrene finally determined as a diagnosis? No. McKinley's medical team identified the stomach pain for the man who had just been shot in the stomach as "indigestion."

On September 13, as gangrene toxified his blood, McKinley collapsed. He died early on the morning of September 14, 1901.

TICKLE THERAPY

Most people figure they've been tickled enough for a lifetime by the time they're, oh, eight or nine years old. After that, tickling usually is an unwelcome experience—the kind you suffer through when your big brother pins you to the floor or when your boyfriend won't stop nudging you while you're in line for the Tilt-a-Whirl.

But in recent years, as part of the explosion of experimentation within the stress-relief industry (an amalgam ranging from massage therapists and acupuncturists to psychoanalysts), tickle therapy has been identified as a method of taking away tension by returning the recipient to the basic pleasures of early childhood…or even infancy.

The thinking behind tickle therapy is that tickling actually feels good if it's done lightly and in a calming environment, using fingers or feathers or other soft-to-the-touch implements. More interestingly, researchers believe that tickling can take a person's subconscious back to his or her first touch interactions as a baby, which often involve parents tickling to induce a smile or laugh.

While tickle therapy remains mostly an anecdotal phenomenon, in 2011 a spa in Madrid called CosquilleArte (translation: "tickle yourself") introduced professionalized tickling—and it proved popular enough to spawn a second location.

URINE THERAPY

It's common knowledge that if you're, say, stranded on a raft adrift in the Pacific Ocean, your best chance to avoid dehydration and death is by drinking your own urine. It's fine to do this—urine is sterile and comprised mostly of H_2O. But there's a select group of people out there who believe that drinking urine is something people should do all the time, even when not lost at sea, and that it's vital for a healthy life.

Urine therapy involves either direct drinking of urine or massaging it into the skin. It's about as alternative as alternative medicine can get, but it's not a modern phenomenon—in ancient Rome, urine was used for teeth whitening. These days, there are a wide variety of practitioners who believe pee is the solution to many of life's problems. For example, former Major League Baseball outfielder Moises Alou eschewed the traditional batting gloves in favor of peeing on his hands to form rock-hard bat-gripping calluses. Madonna once admitted on *Late Night with David Letterman* that she peed on her feet to combat athlete's foot. But probably the most famous proponent of drinking the yellow stuff was former Indian prime minister Morarji Desai. He told Dan Rather on *60 Minutes* that drinking pee was the "perfect" solution for millions of Indians without access to health care (or indoor plumbing).

It's yet to catch on.

MEDICAL VIDEO GAMES

Video games are fun—unless the medical community gets involved. In the early 1990s, software company Raya Systems contracted with pharmaceutical companies to make video games to teach kids about health.

• ***Captain Novolin* (1992).** It's a diabetes-themed game. The plot: The mayor of Pineville has been snatched by aliens, and the titular superhero (named for a brand of insulin) has to rescue him. Captain Novolin must battle temptation—aliens who look like doughnuts and cookies—and keep his blood glucose at a safe level by answering questions about diabetes. (*Captain Novolin* was followed by 1995's *Packy and Marlon*, which starred two diabetic elephants.)

• ***Bronkie the Bronchiosaurus* (1994).** This stars a petite green dinosaur named Bronkie who is tasked with helping rebuild a "wind machine" that was dismantled by the dastardly Mr. Rexo. After all, this machine prevents the city of San Saurian from being swallowed by a deadly dust cloud. Along the way, players learn about the pulmonary system, learn how to recognize attacks, and help Bronkie avoid triggers like cigarette smoke and air pollution.

• ***Rex Ronan: Experimental Surgeon* (1994).** Hey, kids, who wants to play a game in which you have to save a man dying of cigarette-caused lung cancer?

DON'T GO THERE!

And if you do "go there," by which we mean "to developing nations around the world," try not to catch these sicknesses and diseases.

Malaria. The female Anopheles mosquito is native to southeastern Asia and sub-Saharan Africa, and is the carrier of malaria. It's in those regions where the disease is so deadly, killing about a million people annually. Symptoms include muscle aches, chills, and a fever that cycles every couple of days, so just when you think you're better, it comes back…with a vengeance. While there's no malaria vaccine, doctors can prescribe a course of medicines that can prevent malaria from taking hold. To avoid the disease, avoid mosquitoes in southeastern Asia and sub-Saharan Africa: Wear mosquito repellents during the day, use mosquito netting at night, and always wear long sleeves.

Dengue fever. The Aedes mosquito carries this one, and it lives in tropical and subtropical climates, such as the Caribbean, South America, and in the more urban areas of Asia, particularly Taiwan and Singapore. Symptoms of dengue are joint pain, a rash, and other things resembling the flu, up until the patient can go into shock, and die. To prevent getting it, use the same mosquito-aversion techniques one would use to prevent getting malaria–except the medicine. There is no known medicine that can fight dengue fever.

Hepatitis. Both hepatitis A and hepatitis B break down the liver and cause severe abdominal pain, flu-like symptoms, and jaundice. The main difference is that type A clears up after a few months, while type B never goes away and can be fatal. One other difference is that A is easily contractible, spread via food and water in developing nations or anywhere, really, with poor sanitation or food-preparation standards. Type B, however, is spread through sexual contact. Type A has a vaccine–take it before you travel. Type B doesn't have a vaccine.

Cholera. As depicted graphically in the children's novel *The Secret Garden*, cholera is pretty bad–it causes explosive diarrhea and vomiting, and the high fever can ultimately lead to death. It's spread by a bacteria that can be picked up via food and water, so avoid uncooked food and be sure to drink only bottled water if you're traveling through rural Africa or Asia. The good news is that there's a vaccine. The bad news is that experts say it's only about 50 percent effective.

Tetanus. You probably know this word because of the phrase "tetanus shot." Part of the standard regimen of childhood vaccinations, it protects you against tetanus if you were immunized as a child and are up to date with an every-ten-years booster. If you're not, be careful in India and central Africa, where tetanus, or "lockjaw," remains prevalent. "Lockjaw," however, is a misnomer because it also causes muscles to seize and spasm randomly.

HIV and AIDS. Obviously, HIV and AIDS aren't problems only in the developing world. They're merely the most devastating there due to a lack of widespread medical care and education. The disease also doesn't show symptoms for many years, so many carriers don't know they have it. Avoiding it in other countries works the same as in this one: If you're doing heroin, don't share needles (why are you doing heroin?), and never have unprotected sexual contact (why would you have unprotected sexual contact?). Also, try not to commemorate your trip to the developing world with a tattoo or piercing–those needles can carry HIV, too.

Japanese encephalitis. Again, this name is a bit misleading because the disease is common not just in Japan, but in Vietnam, India, Nepal, Malaysia, and Cambodia. It's another mosquito-carried disease, so take the usual anti-mosquito precautions: repellents, nets, and sleeves. Japanese encephalitis is certainly to be avoided–first you think you have the flu…until you're dead. Do yourself a favor before your trip to Asia: Get the vaccine, which is almost 100 percent effective if you get the two doses recommended by the CDC.

+ + +

ORGAN FAILURE. Need a kidney? Good luck. Of the 110,000 Americans on organ donor wait lists, 87,000 need a kidney. Only about 17,000 people in an average year will get one.

AMPUTATIONS: CHEAP, FAST, NOW!

When you're wheeled into surgery, you probably take for granted how fast your procedure seems. An anesthesiologist gives you some gas, you're knocked out, and the next thing you know, you wake up in a recovery room with all the applesauce and off-brand gelatin you can eat.

Doctors, surgeons, nurses, and anesthesiologists take their time to make sure everything goes right, with even a minor surgery taking a full working day or more from start to finish. But prior to the twentieth century, surgery was literally performed as fast as possible. Why? To prevent the patient from dying of shock.

The king of expeditious amputations was a nineteenth-century Scotsman by the name of Dr. Robert Liston. Dr. Liston was able to amputate an entire leg in under three minutes…and this was seen as a good thing. After all, the more time he took, the more time it gave shock to kick in and kill the patient.

But that swiftness came with a price. And that price was accuracy. One would think that, even if one were moving as quickly as possible in a fixed location that something as large as a human leg would be a pretty clear, easy-to-hit target. And one would be wrong.

• On one occasion, Liston swiftly removed a patient's leg, but was so speedy he removed perfectly healthy testicles, too.

• Liston is said to have once amputated a leg in a staggering 28 seconds.

• On another leg amputation surgery, Liston got the leg off, as well as three fingers…of his surgical assistant. He also slashed an observing surgeon for good measure. Unfortunately, infection set in, and that patient died, as did Liston's assistant. And the observing surgeon.

THE DOCTOR IS IN (YOUR WILL)

Decades before Jack Kevorkian, John Bodkin Adams earned the moniker "Doctor Death" for being a suspected serial killer and master manipulator. He convinced his elderly patients (or victims) to change their wills so that he could benefit from their deaths, resulting in a doozy of a conflict of interest.

In 1922 Adams took up a general practice in the sleepy British town of Eastbourne, known as a pleasant retirement location for the well-to-do. Over the course of more than 20 years, he managed to treat 163 patients who each suffered suspicious deaths. Of those, 132 left him money or items in their wills. It was suspected that through his treatment, he managed to "ease the passing" of his patients by keeping them in suspended states of disability through drugs, in at least one case utilizing a cocktail of heroin and morphine to supposedly remedy a woman's discomfort after a stroke. Although that particular patient, Edith Alice Morrell, left Adams out of her will, he still managed to claim a small amount of money, cutlery, and a Rolls-Royce.

By 1956 Adams was one of the wealthiest doctors in England. In July of that year, police were finally tipped off to the dirty dealings of Doctor Death, thanks to an anonymous call from the friend of a victim. The police quickly learned about Adams's preferred technique of administering "special injections" to his patients, which just so happened to never take place in the presence of a nurse; nor did he ever explain to anyone what was in those concoctions.

Adams's trial began in March 1957, splashed across the front pages of newspapers worldwide as the "murder trial of the century." After a mere 44 minutes of deliberation, Adams was found not guilty. He was convicted of a number of lesser charges in a separate trial. But at least he was stripped of his license to practice medicine.

In 1961 he was reinstated as a general practitioner. His authority to prescribe dangerous drugs was restored a year later. He died in 1983 from complications due to an injury suffered while shooting clay pigeons.

✚ ✚ ✚

THANKS FOR THE MEMORIES

A 49-year-old Japanese man went to his doctor in 2008 complaining of abdominal pain. After an MRI, he was informed that he had a large tumor that had to be removed immediately. When the surgeons went in, they didn't find a tumor–they found a surgical towel. It turned out that the towel had been in the man's gut since he'd been treated for an ulcer…in 1983, 25 years earlier. Officials from the hospital that performed the 1983 surgery apologized for the goof and promised to pay all of the man's medical bills, which is probably why he didn't sue.

MASTECTOMY MIX-UPS

When single mom Darrie Eason was told in 2006 that she had an invasive form of breast cancer and needed an immediate double mastectomy, she says she broke down and cried. She was crying again soon afterward, with a combination of relief and outrage, when she learned following surgery that she didn't have cancer after all–her tissue sample had been switched at the lab with that of another patient who did have cancer.

Eason had even sought out a second opinion after her initial diagnosis, but the second doctor examined the same mislabeled tissue the first one had seen, and confirmed the incorrect verdict. It was only after her radical double mastectomy and the first phase of reconstructive surgery that her surgeon sent a sample of her removed tissue to another lab and learned that she was actually cancer-free.

A state investigation suggested that the mix-up probably occurred because the initial lab technician had engaged in "batching," or handling multiple specimens at the same time. Fortunately, once Eason's misdiagnosis had been corrected, the woman whose cancerous tissue sample had been switched with hers–who had been told she was healthy–was able to get the treatment she needed.

A similar lab mix-up two years later resulted in a mastectomy and lymph node removal…on a healthy 28-year-old man. Scott Aprile, who had lost both grandfathers to cancer, went to his doctor after noticing a growth in his right breast. After he received the devastating diagnosis of breast cancer, Aprile's friends began planning benefits for him, donning "Livestrong" bracelets. However, after the surgery, however—which had left a six-inch scar from his armpit to his sternum, and jeopardized his career as a personal trainer—he learned his biopsy results had been switched with those of a woman who was tested the same day.

✚ ✚ ✚

NOT BASED ON A TRUE STORY

In Michael Crichton's 1969 novel *The Andromeda Strain*, a satellite crashes near an Arizona town, which is almost entirely wiped out by a nasty alien virus that had caught a ride to Earth. The only two survivors of the extraterrestrial bug (code-named "Andromeda"), an elderly man and a baby, are rushed to an underground facility where they can be studied. Dr. Mark Hall, the biochemist in charge, determines that Andromeda kills victims with abrupt blood clots or drives them so insane they commit suicide. Then the bug mutates and escapes containment.

In 1996, two British professors hypothesized that the deadly outbreak of mad cow disease was caused by cows eating debris that had fallen from space. Their theory was later refuted.

SECRET EMT JARGON

M.U.H. "Messed-up heart."

P.B.S. "Pretty bad shape."

H.I.B.G.I.A. "Had it before; got it again."

D.F.O. "Done fell over."

C.A.T.S. "Cut all to s***."

S.D.S. "Some dude syndrome." When EMTs are summoned to treat injuries sustained in a fight, it's common for a participant to feign innocence by saying something like "Some dude just came up and started hitting me!"

F.D.W.B. "Fell down; went boom."

C.F.C.P. "Coo-coo for Cocoa Puffs," or a severely mentally ill patient.

F.L.K. "Funny looking kid" (which just seems mean).

T.D.S. "Terminal deceleration syndrome," or in other words, the patient was in a car accident.

High-velocity lead therapy. A gunshot wound.

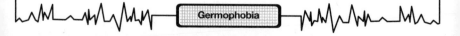

L.O.L.L.O.L. "Little old lady lying on linoleum." That's an elderly woman found dead.

S.N.O.A.D. Short for "severe need of attention disorder." A hypochondriac who calls for ambulances a lot.

I.D. 10 T. On paper, it looks just like the word "idiot," which is what it means.

E.C.U. "Eternal Care Unit," i.e., the morgue.

D.R.T. "Dead right there."

T.B.T.T. "To be toe-tagged, i.e., the patient is dead.

A.R.T. "Assuming room temperature." Dead.

C.T.D. "Circling the drain." Dead.

R.F.D.N. "Ready for dirty nap." Dead.

D.F.L.O.B. "Died from lack of breath." Dead.

T.M.B. "Too many birthdays." Dead.

P.C.T.T.J. "Patient care transferred to Jesus." Dead.

NIP SLIP

We've all been rejected at one time or another. It's practically a rite of passage for most people—getting turned down for a date to the prom, receiving a rejection letter for that job we really wanted, getting turned down for a bank loan, or having a newly implanted breast pop out of our chests. Oh, you mean that's not universal?

Meet Lauren Yardley of Coventry, England. Yardley, unhappy with looking "flat-chested," underwent cosmetic surgery to increase her breast size to a voluptuous DD. A few months after the surgery, however, her right breast began to reject the implant. The phony boob eventually escaped through Yardley's surgical stitches, leaving her feeling dejected and unbalanced. Even worse was that her sister underwent the same procedure with no complications.

"THE PHONY BOOB ESCAPED THROUGH THE SURGICAL STITCHES."

Yardley had to spend seven months looking like an underinflated life jacket before surgeons were able to safely place a new implant. We're happy to report that the procedure was a success and that Yardley, her boobs, and her vanity are now living happily ever after.

THE WANDERING NAVEL

Anyone who has ever hired a contractor to work on their house can tell you the end result doesn't always meet expectations. There might be an unfinished surface here, some dead wiring there. But for Virginia O'Hare, the house was her body, and the shoddy contractors left her belly button in the wrong place.

O'Hare went in for a tummy tuck in 1974 with the expectation she would leave with a "flat, sexy belly" and just a barely noticeable hairline scar. She awoke to find a thick scar, fat oozing out through the openings in the poorly stitched incision, and her navel two inches off-center. "It was like something out of a Frankenstein horror show," she told *People* magazine. Her plastic surgeon, Howard Bellin, was a down-to-earth fellow who hung out with Andy Warhol and boasted of his open marriage in an interview with Barbara Walters. He claimed the wandering navel was the result of an unexpected hernia encountered during the operation.

O'Hare sued and eventually won a settlement of $854,000, but in the process also became a punching bag in the tabloids. In addition to criticism of the size of her award, O'Hare was labeled a plastic-surgery junkie who some claimed had as many as nine previous operations on her nose and eyelids. At least all of those had gone as planned.

PATRON SAINTS OF ASSORTED MEDICAL MALADIES

Denis, Patron Saint of Headaches. This martyr served as the Bishop of Paris in the third century. During a period of Catholic persecution, he was beheaded. According to legend, he stubbornly picked up his own noggin and carried it six miles while still preaching a sermon, which makes him a unique authority on the subject of head pain.

Blaise, Patron Saint of Sore Throats. Blaise was an Armenian doctor who was tortured and killed in the year 316 by persecutors wielding sharp carding combs. As he was first being taken into custody, he reportedly rescued a small child choking on a fish bone.

Catherine, Patron Saint of Sudden Death. Catherine managed to convert the wife of Roman emperor Maxentius to Christianity. In exchange, Maxentius had Catherine beheaded. Invoke her name for protection against any nasty surprises that might result in literally losing your own head.

Domninus of Fidenza, Patron Saint of Rabies. Domninus once served as the keeper of the crown for the Roman emperor Maximian. After converting to Christianity, Domninus went on the run and rode a horse through Piacenza while wielding a cross. He was eventually found and beheaded but, much like

Denis, he supposedly took a miraculous walk afterward with his own cranium in his hands. Keep him in mind if your dog (or horse) ever seems more than a little irritable.

Fiacre, Patron Saint of Hemorrhoids and Sexually Transmitted Diseases. This sixth-century Irish priest wasn't much of a ladies' man. While clearing land to build a hospice, a woman accused him of witchcraft. He was so annoyed that he barred all females from the property. His sainthood is thought to have been inspired by his extreme dislike of the opposite sex.

James, Patron Saint of Arthritis. This saint was one of Jesus' twelve apostles. While being led to his own execution, legend has it that James passed an impoverished man crippled by extreme arthritis and cured him with a simple touch of his hand.

Peregrine of Auxerre, Patron Saint of Snake Bites. Peregrine was born in Italy in the third century and was later sent to convert "heathens" in what is now the Burgundy region of France. After encouraging the locals to give up their pagan idols, Peregrine was beheaded by a seriously irked governor. His sainthood was likely inspired by his commitment to preventing the French from praying to various creepy pagan idols...like snakes.

(DON'T) D.I.Y. PLASTIC SURGERY

The Great Recession put a crimp in many socialites' beauty budgets, never mind the pocketbooks of millions of women obsessed with self-improvement on the cheap. But the grotesque results of one woman's 2009 experiment injecting inferior-grade silicone into her face offered a cautionary tale. People, surgery is complicated business. Leave it to the professionals.

The Midwestern mom (unnamed in press reports) was already well versed in the benefits of silicone, having undergone a procedure in a doctor's office to help fade a facial scar. That injection had cost about $1,000, however, and when the woman wanted to extend those benefits, she thought she could skip the doctor and treat herself. So she found a shady website selling silicone for $10 a bottle, and said she "felt proud" of herself after the self-injections, she said.

She faced a hideous reality in the mirror the next day, however: the non-medical-grade silicone (advertised as a "personal lubricant") had bubbled and expanded under her now-blistered and infected skin. Local doctors had no idea how to help her; eventually she traveled to California (naturally), where a cosmetic surgeon cut out the hardened silicone and the scar tissue that had formed around it.

LET'S FACE IT

In May 2005, Isabelle Dinoire, 38, of Valenciennes, France, was depressed and decided to end it all. So she took a large dose of sleeping pills, and then passed out. When she didn't wake up for several hours, her dog tried to rouse her by licking her and jumping on her. He became more and more alarmed, and in his zeal, he inadvertently mauled Dinoire, destroying her nose, lips, and chin. She finally woke up.

Dinoire recovered from her injuries, but her face was permanently damaged to the point where she could barely eat and couldn't speak at all. Two surgeons from Amiens, France, took an interest in the case and proposed a triangular skin graft. The tissues, muscles, arteries, and veins would be taken from the face of a brain-dead donor and transplanted onto Dinoire. In other words: a partial face transplant.

The skin had to come from a living donor because live tissue ensured proper blood flow; skin from somewhere else on Dinoire's body would be too different in color and texture. The five-hour procedure worked. Dinoire's appearance isn't exactly what it used to be–it's more of a hybrid between her old face and the donor's face–her nose is narrower and her mouth is fuller, for example. She still can't move her lips very well, but she's able to speak, eat, and even smoke again. After all, she's French.

THE WRONG SPERM

Nancy and Thomas Andrews of Long Island, New York, already had a multicultural family–Nancy is from the Dominican Republic and Thomas is Caucasian. They turned to a high-priced Park Avenue fertility clinic, New York Medical Services for Reproductive Medicine, to help them conceive a second child. Thomas dutifully donated his sperm. But when their second daughter, Jessica, was born in 2004 following in-vitro fertilization treatments, she was altogether darker than either of them.

The couple began to suspect that the clinic's embryologist had mistakenly used the wrong sperm, and an at-home DNA test did nothing to assuage their fears. Sure enough, two more professionally administered tests confirmed the awful truth: Thomas wasn't Jessica's biological father. Jessica has "characteristics more typical of African or African-American descent," their lawsuit stated. "While we love Baby Jessica as our own, we are reminded of this terrible mistake each and every time we look at her."

A New York State Supreme Court judge dismissed portions of the Andrews's 2007 suit against the clinic, including their claim of mental distress. "The birth of an unwanted but otherwise healthy and normal child," the judge said, "does not constitute an injury to the child's parents." The suit was eventually settled out of court.

DOCTOR LOVE

It's often said that if you want something done right, you gotta do it yourself. At least that's the personal (and professional) motto of Dr. Cecil Jacobson, a fertility doctor and operator of a reproductive genetics center who took creepy to a whole new level.

Dr. Jacobson spent most of the 1980s using a dumbed-down form of hormone therapy in an attempt to help women get pregnant—with mixed results. A number of his former patients suspected he was a fraud and sued him. And that's when things got really icky.

A number of Jacobson's patients agreed to use sperm from anonymous, screened donors. The problem is that there was no donor program, and many of the children born with his help—estimates range from 15 to 75—were conceived with Jacobson's sperm. There are now potentially dozens of Cecil Jacobsons running around. Yuck.

"THE PROBLEM IS THAT THERE WAS NO DONOR PROGRAM."

After being convicted for perjury and fraud in 1992, Jacobson's lawyer said, "If Cecil made any mistakes, it was in losing his objectivity and trying so hard to get patients pregnant."

Yeah, *that's* where he went wrong.

STILL NO CURE FOR THE COMMON COLD

Annually, Americans alone come down with an estimated one billion colds—that's about three per person—and spend over $4 billion on mostly ineffective cold and cough medications.

The cold is as old as it is common. Egyptian scrolls suggest that people were getting the sniffles at least as far back as 1550 BC. They treated colds with honey, spices, and juniper berries. Today's modern remedies aren't much more sophisticated. While supermarkets have a wide array of supposed cures, from Sudafed to Emergen-C, all they really do is temporarily alleviate symptoms or offer a placebo effect. Sorry, but your mother's chicken soup is just as useless.

Despite all the remedies available, there is no actual cure for the cold quite yet. A big reason is the fact that there's no one single virus called "the cold." There are more than 250 different strains—finding a vaccine to take care of all of those, and its annual mutations, would be profoundly difficult. There's also the simple fact that, for the most part, colds tend to go away on their own after about a week.

Also, nobody dies from a cold, so it's not deemed important enough for the scientific community to gather the manpower, time, and funding to develop a cure. They're busy trying to cure more important and harmful illnesses like diabetes, cancer, and AIDS.

That's not to say that absolutely nobody is working on a cure. Scientists at the Massachusetts Institute of Technology have high hopes for Draco, an experimental drug that causes infected cells to destroy themselves, thus preventing the further spread of a virus. However, it's still in the testing phase and may not be available to the public for another decade or more.

In 2009, researchers at the University of Cambridge announced that they had made a breakthrough during a viral study. They proved that it's possible for an antibody to follow a virus into a cell and kill it before it can cause an infection. Their research may one day lead to the creation of antiviral drugs that could cure not just the cold but also scarier viral illnesses like HIV and hepatitis.

+ + +

DOCTOR? NO.

A 2004 investigation in Italy uncovered a ring of scammers, involving two dental schools in Rome, that sold fake diplomas to dental "students" for as much as $220,000 each. Investigators found evidence of false school-attendance records as well as test answers and term papers provided to students for a fee. Other university staff members were bribed with vacations, gifts, and bonuses to keep them quiet about the scam.

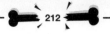

THE UGLY TOOTH

A dentist in Munich, Germany, was sued after deciding to save one of his patients some time–by giving her 14 root canals in one day. The dentist, whose name was not released to the press, fed the woman large glasses of cognac between each drilling during the 12-hour ordeal, telling her it would help ease the pain. Although she probably felt no pain during the operation, she sued because of the enormous pain she suffered for weeks afterward. According to standard dental practices, 14 root canals would normally be performed in several appointments over several weeks. The dentist was ordered to pay her $7,000 in compensation.

• In 2004 twenty dentists in California's Central Valley area were accused of defrauding the state Medi-Cal health system of $4.5 million by performing unnecessary–and cruel–dental work. To lure low-income patients, these dentists went to homeless shelters, shopping malls, and schools offering gift certificates, sweatshirts, and electric toothbrushes. The patients were then given unnecessary dental work, including root canals. Some dentists were accused of holding crying children down in the dental chair and using straps on elderly patients. Then they charged outlandish amounts of money for the work and sent the bills to Medi-Cal.

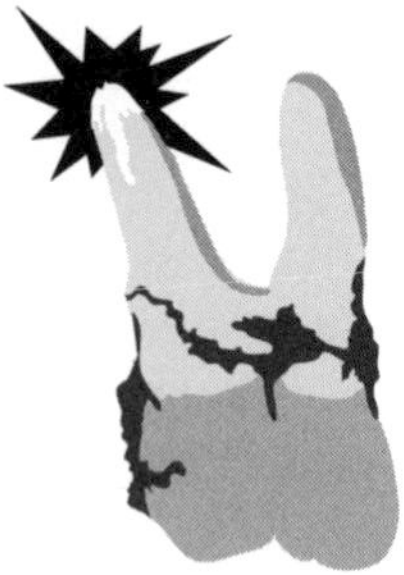

"In every single one of the three hundred files we checked," said an official, "we found fraud." In 2008 the two lead dentists in the scam were sentenced to one year in jail and forced to repay $3 million.

• In June 2004, Dr. Colin McKay of Halton, England, drank six glasses of wine at lunch and then performed a tooth extraction on Andrea Harrison. It didn't go well. It took McKay two tries to inject the anesthetic into her gums, then he started the procedure before Harrison's mouth became completely numb. "I was in a lot of pain and yelled, but he carried on," she said. "Then he seemed to fall over me. I ended up running out." Another dentist finished the extraction; McKay was found guilty of professional misconduct.

• "Dr. Allena Burge pulled teeth so hard and fast, the patients' blood would spray," her assistant, Janet Popelier, told investigators. "Sometimes parts of the jawbone or mandible would break." Why did the Florida dentist have to work so fast? "She was trying to make twelve thousand dollars a day from Medicaid. I saw many half-conscious, bleeding patients led out the back door soon after their surgeries to make room for new patients." Burge was charged with fraud and malpractice. (She even let her 12-year-old son administer anesthesia.) In just four years, she filed more than 57,000 Medicaid claims totaling $6.6 million. No word on the investigation's outcome, but at last report, Burge was still practicing dentistry.

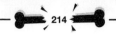

A CASE OF THE BLUES

Wasn't *Avatar* just the coolest movie? Imagine, a whole planet full of exotic people with blue skin! Such a thing is the stuff of wild fantasy, of course. Except that it's really not.

It turns out there's a bunch of people out there right now who have a permanent and literal case of the blues. That's thanks to a condition called *argyria*, which derives from the Greek phrase for "blue skin." Argyria is typically caused by a buildup of microscopic silver compounds in various parts of the body, which then deposit pigments that give the skin a blue hue. Not always, though. Sometimes it manifests as a blue-gray color.

"MICROSCOPIC SILVER COMPOUNDS DEPOSIT COMPOUNDS THAT GIVE THE SKIN A BLUE HUE."

The most notable cases involving argyria come from the use of so-called health products made from colloidal silver (tiny particles of silver suspended in liquid), either mass-produced or homemade, which is touted as a cure-all and immunity booster. The condition is permanent, though not usually life-threatening, but sufferers can face public scorn as well as incessant autograph requests from Blue Man Group fans.

YOU GOT SKULL IN MY STOMACH

If Jamie Hilton, a former Mrs. Idaho, ever decides to enter any more beauty pageants in the future, she has a pretty significant leg up on her fellow contestants when it comes to the skills competition. Singing? Baton twirling? Child's play. Hilton can store her skull in her abdomen. Well, she used to, anyway.

During a fishing trip in June 2012, Hilton slipped and fell 12 feet onto a boulder. In order to alleviate swelling in her brain, doctors removed 25 percent of her skull and implanted it under the skin of her abdomen. Why? It's a spectacular but not uncommon procedure that allows the fragment to remain both sterile and acclimated to the body.

The skull fragment remained in Hilton's belly for 42 days and was successfully reattached. She now has her head in one piece and a damned cool story, too. Just don't ask her to repeat that particular trick.

CLAMPDOWN

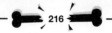

Jeffrey Baber had surgery in 2004 at King-Drew Medical Center in Compton, California. Baber experienced some residual post-surgical pain, as one does. Baber, however, classified his as "extreme pain," and it lasted for 10 days. When Baber returned to the hospital for another (unrelated) surgery, an X-ray revealed that his pain was not normal because his surgical team had left a five-inch metal clamp inside his body.

Meant to hold skin aside or keep organs in place, these kinds of tools are supposed to be removed after they've served their surgical purpose. In fact, it's operating procedure at many hospitals, including King-Drew, for surgeons to count all the tools they use before and after surgery, to make sure the numbers match up. That cuts down on things like metal clamps getting left inside patients. Except, of course, when it still happens.

King-Drew had been cited by state and federal hospital inspectors numerous times in 2004, partly because of the accidental deaths of five patients and for excessive use of electric shock to subdue psychiatric patients. Ironically, the same day Baber filed a $200 million lawsuit against the facility, regulators dropped a threat to pull $200 million in annual Medicare funding to King-Drew, a teaching hospital that primarily treats uninsured patients.

UNCOMBABLE HAIR SYNDROME

Everybody has the occasional bad hair day. But kids with this rare syndrome—identified in the 1970s and also known as "spun-glass hair"—have tresses literally impossible to tame. Manifesting in Caucasian children, the condition causes growth of structurally abnormal hair strands over more than half of the head. These unnaturally stiff bristles are dry, frizzy, and nearly pigmentless, appearing silver-blond, and will stand straight up from the scalp, refusing to lie flat.

It's because of the shape of the hair shaft. European hair strands are typically round in profile; those of African descent have an oval shape to their hair shafts, accounting for tight curls. Uncombable hair, though, shows a longitudinal groove, making a nearly triangular shape in the cross section.

The cause of uncombable hair syndrome is little understood. It does not appear to run in families, although there may be a recessive genetic component. The condition seems to develop spontaneously in children as young as three months. Fortunately, uncombable hair syndrome in itself does not appear to be linked to any more serious medical conditions, and symptoms tend to improve or vanish by adolescence. The most effective treatment appears to be monthly buzz cuts until age 12.

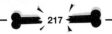

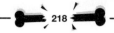

HOW JIM HENSON DIED

In its early stages, pneumonia can feel a lot like the flu. That's what beloved Muppets creator Jim Henson thought he had in early May 1990. After an appearance on *The Arsenio Hall Show*, Henson told his publicist that he was tired, had a sore throat, and that he'd be back to his old self in a few days. A week later, while visiting his father in rural North Carolina, Henson still felt sick. A local doctor examined him and thought he was fine. His prescription: aspirin.

The doctor didn't catch that Henson was infected with streptococcus pneumonia. It's a particularly nasty strain of the virus, but it's treatable if caught in time.

On May 14, Henson returned home to New York and canceled his appointments to stay home and rest. By 2 the next morning, Henson was coughing up blood and wondering aloud to his wife, Jane, if he was dying. She begged him to go to a hospital, but he refused. Why? While rumors at the time persisted that Henson's Christian Science faith prevented him from seeking medical attention, Jane Henson says that he hadn't practiced the faith in years, and that it spoke more to his character: self-sufficient, and never wanting to bother anyone.

"Some people say you can choose the way you die," she told *People* in 1990. "I think he would choose to die with as little trouble to everyone as possible." That same attitude reared as Henson arrived at the hospital. The cab driver dropped the Hensons

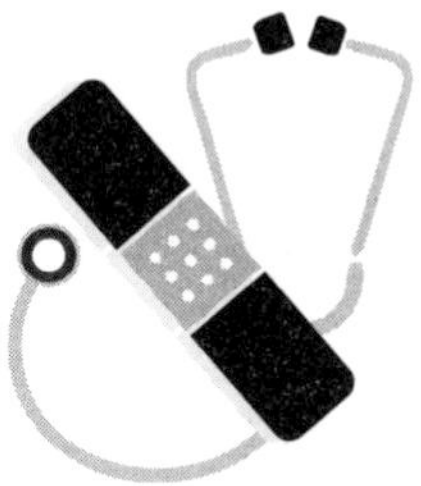

off at the wrong entrance—Henson walked the quarter of a block to the proper door, rather than inconvenience the driver.

Henson was admitted to intensive care. X-rays revealed that he had infections throughout his body and abscesses on his lungs. Henson was in terrible pain and unable to breathe on his own, so by 8:00 a.m., doctors had sedated him and placed him on a ventilator. Throughout that day, Henson was given large doses of antibiotics. They didn't help. Blood uncontrollably spilled into his lungs, he lost his ability to clot, his body went into shock, his kidneys shut down, and he suffered two cardiac arrests.

He never woke up. At 1:21 a.m. on May 16, 1990, Henson's heart stopped for good. He was 53.

Dr. David Gelmont, the director of New York Hospital's intensive care unit at the time and head of the medical team that treated Henson, told the *New York Times* that the strain of pneumonia was severe but not deadly. In fact, he said that Henson probably would have recovered had he gotten to a hospital only "eight hours earlier."

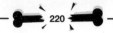

YOUR PETS WANT YOU DEAD

Your dog's sweet kisses will kill you. Bacterial meningitis is a potentially fatal infection characterized by high fever, headache, and nausea. It's transmitted orally. Most people get it by kissing other people, but you can also get it from your dog. In 2011 a Japanese woman contracted the disease after doctors discovered she had the habit of feeding her dog bits of food…from her own mouth. Up to 75 percent of dogs host meningitis bacteria in their mouths, which are, despite popular legend, not cleaner than human mouths.

Your goofy turtles will destroy your kidneys. In 2007 more than 100 people across the United States came down with a salmonella infection, including two friends, aged 13 and 15. Both girls (unnamed in reports) were very sick with fever and cramps, and the older one was hospitalized for eight days with acute kidney failure. The cause? The teens had swum in an unchlorinated pool that was sometimes frequented by two pet turtles. Soon after the outbreak, it was discovered that nearly all the victims had been exposed to pet turtles either directly or indirectly.

Your dog's poop will make you sick. Feces fun fact: Just one gram of dog poop is loaded with 23 million fecal *coliform* bacteria, some of which can make you ill with fever, nausea, bloody diarrhea, or worse. What's worse than bloody diarrhea? One infant's *E. coli* infection was traced back to the family dog. The canine, who might have gotten the bacteria from cattle, had pooped on the living room carpet, and the baby got sick after playing on the floor. The infection quickly progressed into a destructive kidney disorder, which the baby luckily survived.

Your dog's poop will blind you. Roundworms are intestinal parasites that can be passed to humans if animal feces—or soil contaminated with it—accidentally (or on purpose, we suppose) gets in your mouth. Seem unlikely? Each year, 10,000 Americans are horrified to learn their bodies are hosting roundworms, which sometimes appear as spaghetti-like worms in their stool. In 2010 British toddler Aimee Langdon was exposed to roundworms when she got a bit of dog poop in her eye. She was hospitalized the next day. The good news: Treatment prevented the worms from migrating to her brain. The bad news: She was permanently left nearly blind in one eye.

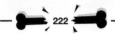

MODERN DAY, OLD DISEASE

Polio. There was once a point when polio killed thousands of U.S. children every year and left tens of thousands with some degree of paralysis. But since vaccinations for the disease became available in the 1950s, polio was eliminated in the U.S. by 1979, and subsequently in most countries around the world. However, as recently as 2013, polio remains endemic in parts of Africa and the Middle East. A 2013 outbreak in Syria has paralyzed at least 10 children, and many doctors are warning that an outbreak in Europe may not be far behind, as vaccination rates are no longer high enough to provide "herd immunity" in countries such as Bosnia and Austria. That means that polio has been so thoroughly eradicated that many countries don't even bother vaccinating for it anymore, which wouldn't be a problem…unless there's an outbreak, such as the one in Syria.

Measles. There aren't many diseases as infectious as measles, which is why in pre-immunization days, nearly every person in the U.S. used to get it. And even with modern medical breakthroughs, between 1953 and 1963, about 450 Americans a year died from measles. Immunizations have nearly eliminated the disease in the U.S., but in recent years, controversies about immunizations, fed by false rumors about a connection between immunizations and autism (see page 54), have led to new measles outbreaks. An outbreak in Indiana in 2005 was linked to parents' refusal to immunize kids, as was a 2008 outbreak in California, and cases in 16 different states in 2013. Today, it's the top cause of death among children... among diseases that could be prevented with a simple shot.

Scurvy. People figured out long ago that scurvy, that old pirate's disease, was the result of vitamin C deficiency. In fact, that's where the term "limey" comes from: In the nineteenth century, the UK Royal Navy added lemon or lime juice to its sailors' rations as a way of combating the disease, which can cause malaise, softening of the gums, pain in the lower extremities, and, eventually, death. But cases are still sometimes reported, including one 2007 case of an otherwise healthy girl whose parents sought treatment after she refused to walk due to pain. The parents explained that they fed the child an organic diet. The problem was the diet which was recommended by the family's church, consisted of a boiled concoction of organic whole milk, barley, and corn syrup—and no vitamin-rich fruits or vegetables. The child was treated with a change in diet and improved dramatically in just three days.

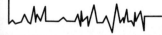

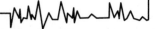

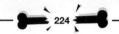

OJ IS THE REAL KILLER

The line between "eating disorder" and "diet fad" is a blurry one. While the United States is becoming more obese, that doesn't mean food isn't still important to eat. But the latest craze among models is especially pernicious: the orange juice diet, which can kill you through malnutrition, in new and exciting ways.

The diet is simple: Drink orange juice. That's it. There are enough pro-OJ screeds online to warm every Florida orange-grower's heart, including one woman who supposedly survived exclusively on orange juice for 51 days. Doctors say it's a miracle she lived to tell the tale, since too much orange juice may lead to hyperkalemia, a severe potassium overdose. It may make your bones strong, but that much potassium also leads to kidney failure and a breakdown in the synapses that allow your brain to control your heart, which is fairly important.

Even that isn't as bad as the most common variant of the OJ diet: supplementing the juice with cotton balls. It apparently leaves you feeling stuffed. Just like a teddy bear. Malnutrition? Check. Hyperkalemia? Check. But that's not all! The bleached synthetic fibers of most cotton balls are potentially poisonous... and can cause deadly intestinal blockages called *bezoars*.

It's probably healthier to just stay fat.

LIFE IMITATES ART

Real-Life *Truman Show*. The 1998 Jim Carrey vehicle *The Truman Show* told the story of a man who slowly realizes his entire life is a fabrication that is being filmed for the entertainment of a large viewing audience. A decade later, doctors in Canada identified five patients who themselves suffered from a delusion that their entire lives were being filmed. The condition was named, appropriately enough, Truman Show Delusion.

Real-Life *Freaky Friday*. You'd be forgiven for thinking that the only serious illness to come out of the *Freaky Friday* films was Lindsay Lohan's slow descent into tabloid insanity. A 40-year-old woman known only in medical journals as "RZ" developed the delusion that she was not only a man, but actually her father, a condition known as *reverse intermetamorphosis*.

Real-life *Outbreak*. In the 1995 thriller *Outbreak*, the Motaba virus originates in Africa and raves rural villages. Symptoms: headache, fever, uncontrolled bleeding, intense vomiting, and certain death. After the virus escapes Africa and infects a small California town, scientists must quickly find a cure. Just weeks after *Outbreak*'s theatrical release, the Ebola virus decimated a community in Zaire with symptoms that include headache, fever, intense vomiting, and death.

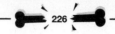

IT'S LEECHCRAFT

Leeches are associated, and rightly so, with the discredited medical practice of bloodletting, in which the cure for any and all ailments was to just get rid of a whole lot of blood. But the thirsty little devils are proving useful in the brave new world of modern medicine–to the point where the FDA has classified them as "live medical devices."

Leeches–bad-boy cousin to your garden-variety garden earthworms–are ideally adapted to their vampiric lifestyle. Their suckerlike mouths conceal three jaws, and they can consume several times their body weight in blood. Doctors are harnessing the very properties that make leeches such effective bloodsuckers.

A leech's saliva contains proteins with anesthetic and anti-inflammatory qualities–making it particularly useful for controlling pain and swelling after reconstructive surgery. The stuff also has an anticoagulant, which prevents clotting and maintains proper blood flow–especially invaluable for surgeries involving the reattachment of body parts with many small blood vessels, like ears or fingers. Such operations have traditionally been tricky because the capillaries in those extremities tended to get closed off with clots, leading to tissue death. Leech venom keeps the capillaries open and the juice circulating, giving severed blood vessels time to get properly reconnected.

STUCK ON YOU

Polymer adhesive, colloquially known as superglue, has sent plenty of people to the emergency room seeking medical help for fingertips that have been accidentally stuck together, or for other mishaps far more painful and embarrassing. Now doctors are finding, in superglue's skin-adhering properties, an alternative to traditional stitches.

It's about proportional response—effectively treating an incision or laceration as noninvasively as possible. Stitches are still the norm for body parts where the skin sees a lot of stretching and compression—joints, for instance. When you've got a gash across the knee, you want a good stout thread holding it all together. But for similar wounds in spots that don't twist around much, like the shin or the forearm, stitches would be overkill.

That's where medical superglue, known as "dermabond," comes into play. Dermabond doesn't go into the wounded tissue itself. Doctors simply clamp the edges of the skin together and apply the glue. Then fiberglass-like microthreads in the epoxy spread across the surface to neatly seal the incision—no bandage required. It's pretty super—and not at all crazy.

SOMETHING SMELLS FISHY HERE

And it's you, if you have *trimethylaminuria*, or TMAU, otherwise known as "fish odor syndrome" or "stale fish syndrome." While seafood is notoriously smelly, that fishy scent usually dissipates over time. Those suffering from TMAU don't have that luxury–the smell never goes away.

The metabolic disorder, which is caused by a genetic mutation, prevents the body from properly breaking down *trimethylamine*, an organic compound that is found naturally in vegetables, meat, and fish when they rot–it is the very thing about fish that makes it smell "fishy." You eat trimethylamine when you eat meat or fish. When someone with TMAU consumes trimethylamine, it builds up in the body, causing a person's sweat, urine, and breath to emit an odor "like rotting fish, rotting eggs, garbage, or urine," as described by the National Institutes of Health. For some reason, more women than men have fish odor syndrome, although overall it's an exceedingly rare disorder; according to one study, fewer than 200,000 people in the U.S. have it.

While fish odor syndrome isn't fatal, it certainly isn't pleasant; unfortunately, there's no cure. What can help people with this syndrome is reducing their consumption of certain vegetables–such as cauliflower, Brussels sprouts, and cabbage–and protein–such as eggs, beans...and seafood.

THE CURATIVE POWERS OF WORM GOO

John of Gaddeden was the first man to serve as court physician to an English monarch, King Edward II. John was also tasked with finding solutions to some of the many health crises plaguing Europe at the time. And, uh, well, the best we can say is that he tried. In 1314 John published the *Rosa Medicinae,* a five-volume omnibus of what he claimed to be a complete record of medical knowledge. Because of John's high rank, the *Rosa Medicinae* was viewed as the definitive medical manual it claimed to be for centuries–it stayed in print until 1595. Here are some of John's "definitive" treatments and cures.

- To cure paralysis, boil a dead dog.

- To treat a poisoned child, sneak goose feces into their food (but don't tell them you did).

- For epileptic seizures, roast a cuckoo, dry it, and turn it into a fine powder. Blow the powder up the nose.

- For a toothache, stick into the gums a needle awash with the secretions of an earthworm.

- To treat mental illness, tie extremities together, soak feet in salt water, pull hair, lightly squeeze toes, make a pig squeal in his ear, cut open a vein in the forehead, draw blood out of the nose with boar bristles, make him sneeze by sticking a feather in his nose, burn human hair under the nostrils, stick a feather down his throat, and shave the back of his head.

THE QUACKIEST OF QUACKS

In the 1820s and 1830s, people had little faith in "scientific" medicine, due no doubt to treatments that were painful and usually produced no results other than infection or death. A new movement of treating illnesses with old folk remedies grew out of the public's fear and distrust of doctors. The medical profession called it "quackery." The word is thought to originate either from the phrase "quicksilver doctor," which refers to the use of highly poisonous mercury as a cure, or from *kwaksalver*, an early Dutch term meaning "someone who prattles about the efficacy of his remedies."

• Before Rogaine and hair plugs came along, men (and some women) dealing with baldness made do with a variety of nonsense treatments. Reuben P. Hall, the creator of the Vegetable Sicilian Hair Renewer, learned his formula in the 1870s from a brilliant but conveniently unnamed European who was down on his luck and sold the formula for some much-needed cash. The secret ingredient? Lead. Nevertheless, various versions of Hall's tonics sold well into the twentieth century.

• The quackery craze stretched into the weight-loss industry in the early 1900s (and some would say it never quite left). One popular "reducing" product: Tapeworm Diet Pills. The pills contained, real, live tapeworms, which, according to the plan, would infest your gut and mess with your intestines, making you lose weight. There are a number of problems with this technique, of course. Tapeworm infestation does lead to weight loss, but a lot of that weight is due to vomiting and diarrhea (not to mention the other side effects of flatulence, nausea, and pieces of worm living inside your body).

• In the 1920s, electromagnetic coils—wires wrapped in insulated belts—were all the rage. According to the hucksters who sold these things, iron in the body helped transport oxygen to cells, and the best way to manipulate iron and move it to all the right places was, of course, magnets. Supposedly, the electrified belts could also supercharge the iron, thus making users look and feel years younger. It was even said to cure cancer.

• In 1928, Philip Ilsey introduced his coil, the Theronoid Electromagnetic Solenoid. Its classy imitation leather coating, along with extensive radio advertising, made it a hit among ladies, who were convinced that a daily three-to-five-minute treatment could cure everything from constipation to "aches." Ilsey's detractors dubbed it the "Magic Horse Collar." The Federal Trade Commission intervened in 1933 and banned further ads promoting the Theronoid as a therapeutic device.

CARTER'S LITTLE (LIVER) PILLS

Perhaps you've heard your grandparents invoke Carter's Little Liver Pills as a superlative of quantity (e.g., "That fellow's got more problems than Carter's has Little Liver Pills"). Undoubtedly, the folks at Carter-Wallace have sold a lot of their little pills since introducing them in the 1880s. But what are they supposed to do, anyway?

An 1887 newspaper ad declared Carter's pills as a cure for "torpid liver," an ailment that sounds euphemistic if not downright made-up. The associated symptoms–sluggishness, bloated feeling, headache, anxiety–are also suspiciously vague and common, and certainly not suggestive of any known liver disorder. The FDA agreed, and in 1943 disputed the efficacy of Carter's Little Liver Pills.

After a challenge dragging on for 16 years, a court order forced Carter's to drop any reference to the liver from its promotions. There were no fines or penalties, though, and the product stayed on the market–as "Carter's Little Pills."

And Carter's could continue to tout the pills as a remedy for torpor, bloating, and nerves–but only when these symptoms were due to constipation. The product is still available, in fact, having been rebranded yet again with the more accurate (but less memorable) name "Carter's Laxative."

BUTT WHY?

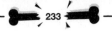

A real bummer. In 2007, 26-year-old Dean Sims underwent an operation at Woolwich Hospital in London. Reason: to remove a harmless, although painful, abscess from his left buttock. It was supposed to be a routine surgery, with no overnight stay even required–the worst side effect was that sitting would be a little painful for a few days. So Sims returned home and discovered, the first time he gingerly sat down to use the bathroom, that he really couldn't sit down to use the bathroom: His buttocks had been improbably and unnecessarily taped shut with surgical tape. He called the hospital to complain, but long lines meant he'd have to wait a day to have the bandage removed properly by a nurse because "gangrene could set in" if he attempted the removal himself.

A hole new world. "Johanna L." checked into the Hochfranken-Klinik in Münchberg, Germany, in March 2008 to have knee surgery. But when she woke up in the recovery room, her knee hadn't been operated on…and she felt a strange breeze blowing up the back of her gown. She called a nurse, who informed Johanna that she had been given an artificial anus (which is apparently a real thing). Apparently, there was a records mix-up: The patient who was suffering from severe incontinence got knee surgery; Johanna got that patient's new anus. She sued the hospital, and the doctors were suspended. (But, hey: free artificial anus!)

THE DIRT ON CLEANLINESS

Since 1860, the average American life span has doubled. Though much of the credit for that goes to observably obvious progress in medical intervention, much more is due to advances in sanitation, driven by our evolving standards of cleanliness.

We often think of cleanliness as an objective state—either you are or you aren't—but notions of sanitation are socially constructed. And those notions take time to spread. Our modern concept of proper hygiene was propagated by the tireless educational efforts of nurses. Beginning in the 1890s, corps of visiting nurses traveled to slums and farm country alike (into conditions that we would find unthinkably squalid) to instruct young families in proper, and then revolutionary, sanitary practices.

You might see pictures of Third World children with insects crawling on their faces, or marketplaces where the meat swarms with flies, and think, *How can they stand that?* Turns out they have to be taught *not* to stand it. In much of the world, crawling bugs are simply a part of the environment—pests, sure, but scarcely worth complaining about, despite their role as carriers of contagious disease. Even today, relief agencies distributing mosquito netting in the developing world also need to educate (or, less charitably, indoctrinate) people with different standards of cleanliness to share the West's aversion to insects.

As it happens, though, that aversion is fairly recent, even in the industrialized West. It was not until the 1920s that window screens became commonplace. The attitudinal shift has been swift and complete—so much so that the mere sight of an insect in the house will send many children into hysterics.

Since notions of cleanliness are culturally specific, there's a natural tendency to think of our own standards as the correct ones. Few Americans, for instance, would consider a bidet to be an indispensable accessory, but no European bathroom is complete without one. It seems like overkill to us. Then again, tenth-century English chroniclers thought the invading Vikings were sort of weird because they—unlike the English—would wash their faces every single day.

As our standards of sanitation evolve, though, nature pushes back. The rise of so-called antibiotic-resistant "superbugs" is a direct result of natural selection interacting with overaggressive cleansing regimens. Perhaps, in order to remain robust and keep the bugs at bay, the human species should learn to put up with a little more filth in the environment. Sure, it would be an adjustment, but it wouldn't be the first time we've redefined our notions of "clean enough."

DRESS FOR THE JOB YOU WISH TO HAVE

In January 2004, Norman Hutchins walked into a hospital in York, England, and explained to a staffer that he was going to a costume party dressed as a doctor. Could he borrow a surgical gown, a mask, and some rubber gloves? The staffer was cooperative at first, but when Hutchins asked her to accompany him into the restroom, she became suspicious. She called police.

The staffer's suspicions were quickly confirmed. Hutchins was a fetishist with an obsession for surgical clothing. For 15 years, he'd been visiting various English and Welsh hospitals with invented excuses like "costume parties," "stage plays," "animal experiments," and "charity fun runs," hoping to con hospital staff into giving him free masks, gloves, and scrubs.

Hutchins had managed to avoid the notice of the National Health Service until they set up a new computer system and began compiling statistics nationwide. In the first five months alone, Hutchins racked up 47 different incidents at hospitals all over England. That's when he made British medical history: In June 2004, he became the first person ever to be banned from every public and private hospital, medical office, and dental office in the country. (He can still get treated for a genuine medical emergency, but if he fakes it, he faces five years in prison.)

MANIMAL INSTINCT

Do you know where your newly transplanted organ came from? It might have come from a sheep. Or a pig. In March 2007, Professor Esmail Zanjani of the University of Nevada-Reno announced that he had successfully injected sheep fetuses with human stem cells. The result: sheep that grew partially human organs. Some had livers, for example, that were made up of as much as 40 percent human liver cells.

Zanjani hopes the research may one day lead to sheep being raised only for the human organs in their bodies—which could be transplanted into humans who need them. The scientists could conceivably create sheep that are tailor-made for specific people. For example, a sheep could be injected with your bone marrow in order to grow organs suitable just for you—no organ rejection drugs required.

Jeffrey Platt, director of the Mayo Clinic Transplantation Biology Program in Rochester, Minnesota, performed similar human stem-cell injections into fetal pigs, and now has a group of pigs that have both pig blood cells and human blood cells running through their veins. But it gets weirder: Some of the blood cells are both. Their DNA contains both human and pig genes. Platt hopes the work might lead to pigs being raised for their human blood and organs, but there are several hurdles, including the fact that some porcine viruses can be passed on to humans.

AN UNHEALTHY ATTACHMENT

Ten-year-old Candace Newmaker had been having trouble bonding with her adoptive mother, so, under the supervision of an "attachment therapist," she was swaddled in a flannel blanket and forced into a "birth canal" of couch cushions as five adults pushed on her from outside. The idea was that Candace would emerge from this birth-approximating ordeal "reborn" to her new mom, thus sealing the emotional bond between them. Instead, after 70 minutes of being pushed through and smothered by couch cushions, Candace died of asphyxiation.

This horrific case is an example of Attachment Therapy, a movement that claims to help parents connect with their troubled adoptive children. Now, it's true that adopted children are at heightened risk for psychological issues. The DSM-IV, the diagnostic handbook of the mental health profession, recognizes Reactive Attachment Disorder (RAD), in which early childhood trauma leads to later difficulties in forming emotional connections. There are real therapies for RAD, but none of them are quick or easy, and all of them require parents to acknowledge their responsibilities by exercising patience, setting expectations, and, above all, managing their own anger. By acting, in other words, like parents.

Attachment Therapy, catering entirely to the sensibilities of parents, lays blame for the emotional distress on the afflicted child. AT encourages parents to view their children as lying, manipulative—even evil. AT advocates warn that RAD can blossom into full-on psychopathy, telling parents in so many words that their children are serial killers waiting to happen. Even if children are well-behaved and happy around people other than their parents—with teachers, say—that's a warning sign.

The "therapy" itself consists of brutal physical and emotional stimuli aimed at breaking a child's will and reducing him or her to a state of helpless dependence, resulting in absolute submission to parental authority (which, sure, might happen) and true love and trust between parent and child. This theory might be funny—if it weren't so horrible, or occasionally deadly.

✦ ✦ ✦

CROUTON-GATE

In 2004 the Queen's Medical Centre in Nottingham, England, suspended its top brain surgeon, Dr. Terence Hope, because he failed to pay for a bowl of soup and some croutons in the hospital cafeteria. The hospital had a 39-day waiting list for brain surgeries at the time. Hope, who had been with the hospital for 18 years and denied stealing any food, was back on the job five days later. A hospital spokesperson said that they had investigated the alleged theft, and conceded that it had been a misunderstanding.

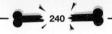

THE DOWNSIDE OF HEALTHY THINGS

The annual checkup. Making sure you're in tip-top shape by getting a yearly physical is a good idea, right? Not so fast: Department of Health and Human Services studies found "no evidence that routine pelvic, rectal, and testicular exams made any difference in overall survival rates for those with no symptoms of illness." In addition, common diagnostic tests, such as examining cholesterol or blood pressure, "need not be done every year."

• **Taking your multivitamins.** Getting your recommended daily dose of calcium, iron, and vitamin C is important, but too much can be a bad thing. Consume too much vitamin C and you might get diarrhea. Zinc can help your immunity, but too much can actually reduce immunity or lead to heart problems. More than enough selenium can cause hair loss; vitamin B_6 overdoses may cause nerve damage.

• **Drinking water.** Eight glasses (or 64 ounces) of water a day is a good, if slightly excessive, way to keep dehydration at bay (see page 46). But people who've gone overboard and imbibed excessive amounts of H_2O run the risk of water intoxication, an actual condition in which electrolyte balance is thrown out of whack. The consequences can be deadly—everything from mental confusion and seizures to brain damage and even death. Yes, from water.

TRENCH FOOT

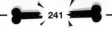

Of the horrors unleashed by World War I, trench foot was relatively mild, but surprisingly ubiquitous. There was a time when every family had that one uncle who could only wear white socks.

Trench foot was first identified in 1914. A lingering fungal infection of the toes, it flourished in the cold, muddy conditions of the battlefield trenches, causing itching, blistering, and pain—a sort of athlete's foot run amok. Military authorities at first dismissed the condition as a dodge, an excuse for work-shy soldiers to avoid their duties. (These were the same authorities, remember, who would deny the reality of post-traumatic stress, then order their enlisted men to be shot for cowardice.) But trench foot could quickly escalate to gangrene if left untreated, and many soldiers lost toes to amputation; estimates indicate 20,000 trench foot–related casualties among the British Army in 1914 alone.

Improved sanitary conditions in the trenches, coupled with simple preventive measures such as petroleum jelly and clean socks, helped control the problem as the war proceeded. But trench foot has resurfaced in later conflicts, and its aftereffects—including a propensity to toenail fungus and an allergic sensitivity to most kinds of dye—would follow many sufferers for the rest of their lives.

KILLER NURSE

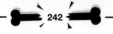

The best nurses display compassion and empathy when dealing with patients. Jane Toppan, a nurse in New England in the late nineteenth century, decidedly did not fall into this category: The cold-hearted caretaker admitted to killing 31 patients in her care over the course of several decades. Some suspect the actual victim count was even higher.

Toppan's murderous methods involved poisoning—specifically by using atropine (a drug derived from deadly nightshade) and morphine—and her victims ranged from those in hospitals to elderly patients who hired her as an in-home private nurse. Her undoing came after four members of the Davis family died within weeks of each other in 1901, all after having been treated by Toppan. The husband of one such victim, Mary Gibbs, insisted on an autopsy, which revealed deadly levels of morphine and atropine in her system.

During Toppan's trial—which unearthed the fact that her father and sister had spent time in insane asylums—she didn't help her case: she reportedly claimed, "That is my ambition, to have killed more people—more helpless people—than any man or woman who has ever lived." Unsurprisingly, she was found to be insane and spent the rest of her life in the Taunton Insane Hospital, where she passed away at age 84.

ANGEL OF DEATH

End-of-life decisions are difficult for the family of a terminal patient. So for ten years, a nurse at a hospital in Glendale, California, was generous enough to make those decisions for his patients.

Efren Saldivar was a respiratory nurse at Glendale Adventist Medical Center. In 1998, police questioned him after several co-workers reported his suspicious behavior. Saldivar confessed to killing 50 patients by administering drugs to stop their breathing, but said he did so as an act of mercy. Soon after, he denied his confession. Police were forced to exhume 20 of the more than 1,000 patients who had died during Saldivar's shift. Six of those showed traces of the drug Saldivar allegedly used.

In 2002, the "Angel of Death" pled guilty to those six counts of murder to avoid the death penalty. But at his sentencing, the judge unsealed a second confession in which Saldivar claimed to have killed well over 100 patients, including some at two other hospitals where he moonlighted. In that confession, he also said he killed patients simply to lighten his workload, and likened it to shoplifting. "After that moment, you don't think about it the rest of the day, or ever," he said. To this day, nobody knows exactly how many victims he claimed.

A LITTLE STING

A honeybee is like a good cocktail: sweet in the tongue, but with a sting in its tail. A single sting from a bee defending its hive–and since the wee buggers travel in swarms, a victim hardly ever gets just a single sting–can be uncomfortable at best, causing a sharp burning pain that lasts long after the barbed stinger with its venom sac is removed. For people allergic to bees, that sting can trigger life-threatening anaphylactic shock. Even the fact that the bee dies after stinging is little consolation.

So the idea of getting stung intentionally, for one's health, is a bit surprising. But scientists have found in the painful toxins in honeybee venom a powerful anti-inflammatory compound that can actually help to alleviate severe pain in patients suffering from several autoimmune disorders, including multiple sclerosis and rheumatoid arthritis.

"SCIENTISTS HAVE FOUND IN THE PAINFUL TOXINS OF HONEYBEE VENOM A POWERFUL COMPOUND."

It's common for doctors administering medicine to warn their patients, "This is going to sting a little," but never before has it been so literal.

ITCHY STITCHES

The feeling of insects crawling on your skin is a symptom of itching. The reality of insects crawling on your skin can be a method for stitching.

For centuries, traditional cultures, from the Maasai of Africa to the rainforest tribes of South America, have used ants to suture minor wounds. The technique is even described in a classic Sanskrit medical text, the *Sushruta Samhita*. And now the procedure is being revived for the modern world. Hooray?

Ants have large, powerful mandibles that can penetrate the flesh at the edges of a wound as effectively as a suture needle. Doctors use special sterile, "medical-grade" ants to nip the edges together. After biting, the ants' heads are severed from their bodies, causing the jaws to lock in place–creating, in effect, an organic surgical staple that will dissolve within a week or two. Done properly, the ant-suture method actually promotes cleaner healing and reduces risk of infection.

That's of little consolation to the ants, though, who go into the procedure expecting a tasty meal and end up getting decapitated for their curiosity.

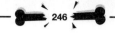

PUTTING THE "BYE" IN ANTIBIOTICS

In 1918 the Spanish flu killed more people than died in the entirety of World War I. Between 50 million and 100 million people succumbed, roughly 5 percent of the earth's entire population at the time. So it was nice when scientists discovered antibiotics shortly thereafter! Some of the most effective disease killers, antibiotics (such as penicillin and amoxicillin) have helped prevent infections like the flu from turning into devastating global pandemics. It's really too bad that they *just* stopped working.

Antibiotics work by killing bacteria, while usually leaving safe, healthy human cells mostly unharmed (as opposed to more extreme disease-and-healthy tissue-killing treatments like radiation or chemotherapy). They're basically poison for bacteria, but over the past 70 years, the bacteria have developed a tolerance.

Mutation guarantees that a small percentage of bacteria would eventually become antibiotic-resistant. But when antibiotics have been added to everything from hand soap to animal feed (which gets passed on to the humans who eat those animals), mutation and evolution accelerated. While many strains died, those that didn't became supergerms unkillable by traditional drugs.

JAM SESSION

In 2009, Denise Joyce Reed began working as an RN at Great Western Hospital in Swindon, a city 80 miles west of London. Shortly thereafter, her fellow nurses began noting her flippant, and often completely indifferent, attitude when it came to treating the patients in her care. While conducting her rounds in January 2010, a patient told her that another patient's mouth was bleeding. A feasible, even common situation in a hospital...but Reed told the Good Samaritan that the blood coming out of the other patient's mouth was just "jam."

Fortunately another, more careful, nurse overheard the conversation and discovered that the patient's chin was indeed covered in blood—and not delicious jam—that had been oozing out of his gums. He later underwent surgery to repair the wound in his mouth.

Reed later claimed that it was all an honest mistake. She said that the patient did have *some* jam on his chin, having had some with his breakfast, and that any bleeding must have happened after she left his room. Reed's supervisors didn't buy her story, and she was placed on leave, then fired. Later, she got her job back on appeal...but she then dispensed the wrong medication to a patient, and also failed to notify another nurse that a patient had had a heart attack. Reed then lost her job for good.

IRON LUNGS

The iron lung—also known as the tank respirator or negative pressure ventilator—saved the lives of countless polio patients during the disease's twentieth-century heyday. In essence, these devices were bulky, airtight, cylindrical contraptions that used air-pressure shifts to induce breathing in people who couldn't do so on their own, whether due to muscle paralysis (a common, famous effect of polio) or another malady.

The origin of the device's technology dates back to 1670, when a British scientist named John Mayow figured out the concept of respiration. He demonstrated this idea by manually inflating and deflating a bladder attached to a bellows—thereby mimicking breathing and creating the idea of artificial respiration, or external negative pressure ventilation.

Doctors eventually adopted this simple concept when they were looking for a way to treat victims of coal-gas poisoning or polio patients who were stricken by muscle paralysis in their chests. But it took the efforts of two Harvard professors, Philip Drinker and Louis Agassiz Shaw, in the late 1920s to finally make a functional version that could successfully treat polio patients. Known initially as the "Drinker respirator," this early iron lung used vacuum cleaners and an electric motor to get results.

Soon after, John Emerson improved the device and made it less expensive—although in the 1930s, during the height of the Great Depression, an iron lung cost about $1,500, roughly the cost of a home at the time.

Either way, the machine was a much-needed panacea for a serious epidemic: By 1952, there were 21,000 Americans who had been paralyzed in some way by polio, and 3,000 had died. While respirator technology has come a long way in the last several decades–the machines are suitcase-sized and affordable these days, for example–there are still a small number of polio patients using iron lungs today. “It feels wonderful, actually, if you’re not breathing well,” Oklahoma resident Martha Lillard told NBC News in November 2013. “When I was first put into it, it was such a relief. It makes all the difference when you’re not breathing.”

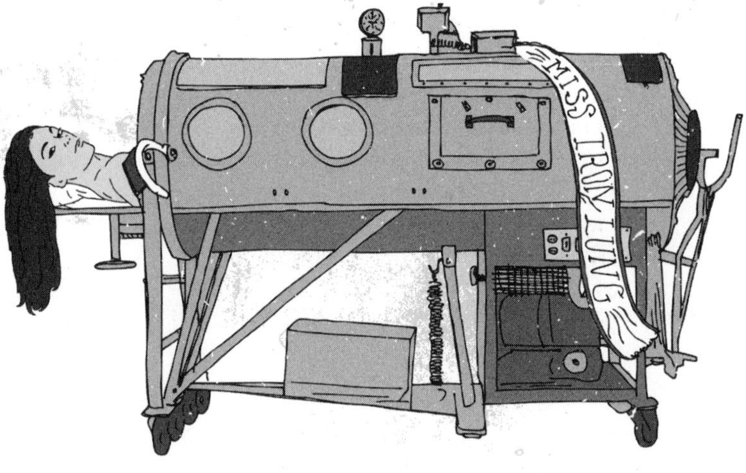

TWO TRUE EMT ADVENTURES

Mark Musarella, 46, of Staten Island, New York, was an emergency medical technician with the Richmond University Medical Center. When he was called to an apartment where a 26-year-old woman had been murdered, he took a photo of the dead body with his cell phone and posted the photo on his Facebook page. One of Musarella's friends saw the photo and called the hospital where he worked. He was immediately fired, then arrested on charges of official misconduct and disorderly conduct. He was sentenced to 200 hours of community service. Musarella—a former highly decorated NYPD detective—also lost his EMT license.

• In March 1987—on Friday the 13th, no less—a man identified only as a 30-year-old Swede began choking on a piece of steak while at a restaurant in Norrkoping, Sweden. Paramedics could not dislodge the steak, and the man was dying in the back of the ambulance as it rushed to the hospital. Then, according to a Swedish newspaper account, "a few hundred yards from the hospital, the ambulance collided with a car. It was not a serious collision and no one was hurt. But the impact dislodged the chunk of beef, and the man resumed breathing."

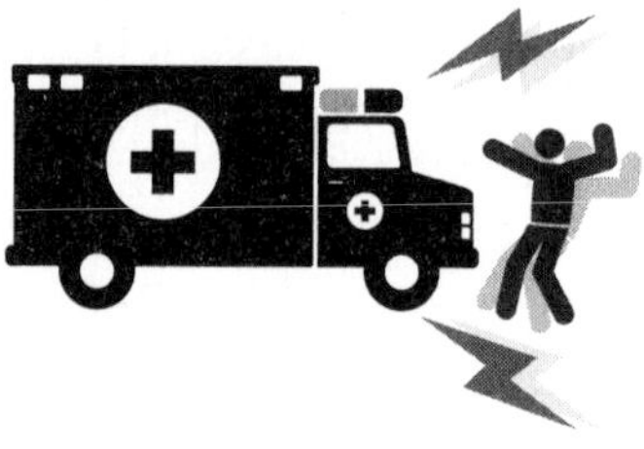

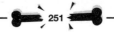

THE HOT NEW DISEASE

Most diseases have been around for centuries or were at least identified a long time ago, such as cancer or gout. Not "progressive inflammatory neuropathy," which is relatively new and totally terrifying.

In February 2008, a translator at a medical clinic in Minnesota noticed that three different Spanish-speaking workers at a nearby pork-processing plant (okay, a slaughterhouse) had come in with complaints of fatigue and burning sensations in their limbs. A consult with a doctor revealed that 12 slaughterhouse employees had similar symptoms, as did some employees of a slaughterhouse in Indiana.

As it turns out, all of the victims worked in similar locations in their plants: near the "head table"...where the pigs' brains are removed from the carcasses with high-pressure air hoses. (The brains are then sold to food markets in Asia.) Researchers from the Centers for Disease Control in Atlanta are still conducting studies on the disease, but they believe it may be a brand-new illness. How do they think people catch it? By inhaling tiny pieces of pig brain, like those floating in the air at slaughterhouses. The body produces antibodies against the foreign brain bits, and the antibodies then attack the body's own nerve fibers—resulting in this neurological illness.

NOTABLE CLEAN FREAKS

Howard Hughes. The name of the famed aviator and baron of industry is synonymous with *mysophobia*, a.k.a. germophobia. Hughes kept the condition in check throughout most of his life, but it got out of hand after he nearly died in a 1946 plane crash. Shortly thereafter, Hughes started locking himself away for months at a time in what he claimed were "germ-free" hotel penthouses. He reportedly wore Kleenex boxes as slippers, and he stuffed the tissues into the edges of windows to keep germs from coming in. Hughes wrote his assistants incredibly detailed notes instructing them to keep their clothing spotless, to use brand-new knives to open his Kleenex boxes, and never to come within four feet of him.

Donald Trump. What terrifies the man with America's most terrifying toupee? Germs. He says it's a symptom of obsessive-compulsive disorder (OCD). "The Donald" reportedly refuses to touch the ground-floor button in elevators and loathes shaking hands with people, especially teachers. "According to a new study, teachers have the germiest jobs," Trump said in 2006. "They have seventeen thousand germs per square inch on their desk. That's ten times the germ rate of those in other professions." His fear of shaking hands is reportedly a major reason why he decided not to run for president in 2012.

Howie Mandel. When the comedian hosted the game show *Deal or No Deal,* he refused to touch palms with contestants unless he was wearing latex gloves. While interviewing Marshall Faulk on the NFL Network a few years ago, he screamed and allegedly ran off to wash his hands for 20 minutes after the former running back abruptly shook his right hand. Mandel keeps his head shaved because it helps him feel cleaner, and he's been known to freak out during the filming of episodes of his current show, *America's Got Talent*, when contestants do something that he finds icky. Mandel wrote about his lifelong battles with OCD and mysophobia in his 2009 memoir, *Don't Touch Me*.

More mysophobics:

- **Michael Jackson** didn't wear those surgical masks everywhere he went to provide a little bit of privacy. Nope–he was deathly afraid of germs.

- **Billy Bob Thornton** has several OCD-related behaviors, including an aversion to metal eating utensils. Convinced they just aren't clean, he brings his own plastic knives and forks to restaurants.

- **Jessica Alba** thoroughly sprays anti-bacterial Febreze on hotel bed linens.

- **Gwyneth Paltrow** brings her own brushes and combs to hairdressers.

PURELL WON'T SAVE YOU NOW

It's rare to enter an office building, grocery store, or hospital without immediately encountering a giant dispenser of hand sanitizer. These ubiquitous bottles of germ-preventing goo, oil, foam, or lotion (Purell brand or otherwise) have taken some criticism for not being as effective in killing bacteria as their manufacturers claim; the label generally promises "99 percent" kill-ability. But that doesn't fully explain why hand sanitizers are not fully effective.

Triclosan is an antibacterial and antifungal agent found in many hand sanitizers. Some experts say that triclosan provides the same amount of protection against illness-causing germs as a simple soap-and-water hand washing. But more troubling is that triclosan is known to cause muscle loss in animals as well as, horribly ironic as it is, weakened immunity. Even worse, the same bacteria that triclosan is trying to prevent from spreading has been found to become easily resistant to the agent over time.

However, all is not lost in the world of hand sanitizers. Doctors still recommend sanitizers that are comprised of at least 60 percent alcohol…if you don't have access to soap and water. So unless you're taking hourly Purell breaks so you can strike up a conversation with the cute receptionist, you can probably just use what's in the office bathroom.

UNCLE JOHN'S BATHROOM READER CLASSIC SERIES

Find these and other great titles from the Uncle John's Bathroom Reader Classic Series at *www.bathroomreader.com*.

Or contact us at:

Bathroom Readers' Institute
P.O. Box 1117
Ashland, OR 97520
(888) 488-4642

THE LAST PAGE

FELLOW BATHROOM READERS:

The fight for good bathroom reading should never be taken loosely—we must do our duty and sit firmly for what we believe in, even while the rest of the world is taking potshots at us.

We'll be brief. Now that we've proven we're not simply a flush-in-the-pan, we invite you to take the plunge:

Sit Down and Be Counted! Log on to www.bathroomreader.com and earn a permanent spot on the BRI honor roll!

Well, we're out of space, and when you've gotta go, you've gotta go. Tanks for all your support. Hope to hear from you soon.

Meanwhile, remember...

KEEP ON FLUSHIN'!